The
Referral Engine

The
Referral Engine

TEACHING YOUR BUSINESS
TO MARKET ITSELF

John Jantsch

Portfolio

PORTFOLIO

Published by the Penguin Group

Penguin Group (USA) Inc., 375 Hudson Street, New York, New York 10014, U.S.A.
Penguin Group (Canada), 90 Eglinton Avenue East, Suite 700, Toronto, Ontario,
Canada M4P 2Y3 (a division of Pearson Penguin Canada Inc.)
Penguin Books Ltd, 80 Strand, London WC2R 0RL, England
Penguin Ireland, 25 St. Stephen's Green, Dublin 2, Ireland (a division of Penguin Books Ltd)
Penguin Books Australia Ltd, 250 Camberwell Road, Camberwell, Victoria 3124, Australia
(a division of Pearson Australia Group Pty Ltd)
Penguin Books India Pvt Ltd, 11 Community Centre, Panchsheel Park,
New Delhi – 110 017, India
Penguin Group (NZ), 67 Apollo Drive, Rosedale, North Shore 0632, New Zealand
(a division of Pearson New Zealand Ltd)
Penguin Books (South Africa) (Pty) Ltd, 24 Sturdee Avenue, Rosebank,
Johannesburg 2196, South Africa

Penguin Books Ltd, Registered Offices: 80 Strand, London WC2R 0RL, England

First published in 2010 by Portfolio, a member of Penguin Group (USA) Inc.

10 9 8 7 6 5 4 3 2 1

Copyright © John Jantsch, 2010
All rights reserved

LIBRARY OF CONGRESS CATALOGING IN PUBLICATION DATa
Jantsch, John.
The referrals engine : teaching your business to market itself / John Jantsch.
    p. cm.
Includes index.
ISBN 978-1-59184-311-5
1. Business referrals.   2. Viral marketing.   3. Word-of-mouth advertising.   I. Title.
HF5438.25.J63 2010
658.8'72—dc22   2009049521

Printed in the United States of America

To all the brave, smart, dedicated, adventurous, passionate, creative, and adaptive small business owners making this world a better place to live, work, and grow.

Acknowledgments

I would like to start by acknowledging my family for encouraging, supporting, and humbling me at all times.

The readers, subscribers, and customers who participated in this project either directly, by providing their stories to this work, or indirectly, by passing a story on or referring a friend.

The Duct Tape Marketing Coach Network, including Cidnee Stephen and Joe Costantino for putting your faith in the powerful idea of a shared network.

The authors and business professionals that inspire me to keep getting better at my craft including Seth Godin, Brian Clark, Guy Kawasaki, David Meerman Scott, Chris Brogan, and Anita Campbell.

David Moldawer for bringing this project to Portfolio and thoughtfully making these ideas come to life on the printed page.

Steve Hanselman of LevelFiveMedia, my friend, literary agent, and constant supporter.

The great folks at Federated Media, whom I consider my greatest strategic partner.

Rachel Burd for a level of copy editing I wish I carried around with me daily.

Contents

The
Referral Engine

Introduction

This book is about referrals, but it offers much more than just another set of tips and tricks for generating new leads. *The Referral Engine* offers a systematic approach to generating word of mouth as a comprehensive marketing strategy. In a larger sense, it proposes a new and better way of doing business.

There was a time when marketers would simply create a product or brand, broadcast a compelling message, and send the sales folks out to hunt down new business. Over the past few years, in large part due to the explosion of online tools and networks, customers and prospects are now active participants in the creation of products, services, brands, positioning, messages, and subsequent buzz—for good or bad.

This book will show you how to craft a strategy that compels customers and partners to voluntarily participate in your marketing, to create positive buzz about your products and services to friends, neighbors, and colleagues. While it may feel a bit odd to suggest that you can actually compel someone to perform a voluntary act, you'll find that the pull of a fully developed Referral Engine is so strong that your brand supporters will feel as though they have no choice but to sing your praises.

One warning before we begin: Building the ultimate referable business is not a weekend project. It will require you to look at your business and marketing in an entirely new way. If you come along for this ride, you will need to completely rethink your current marketing strategy, dispense with much widely accepted business "wisdom," and possibly alter the foundations of your business model.

I'd like to share a little experience of my own to help get you in the Referral Engine frame of mind.

One day my wife and I hit a sale at the outdoor gear retailer REI. During the trip she found a coat that she loved and bought it. A few weeks later, we went to an outdoor event and she took the opportunity to wear her new coat. As we went out the door she reached into the pocket and found a little slip of paper.

She pulled the slip out fully expecting something along the lines of "Inspected by #48." Instead, the note read "You are a goddess!" That simple, unexpected message made her day. Of course, we both wondered, who made this coat? I checked the manufacturer's Web site and discovered a very cool little garment company called Isis (www.isisfor women.com), located in Burlington, Vermont.

This creative act, unrelated to the quality, cut, or color of the coat in question, compelled us both to think fondly of this company and voluntarily refer them to anyone who would listen. Something I'm doing right now.

Let's get started on your Referral Engine, shall we?

CHAPTER 1

The Realities of Referral

Despite what some might suggest, there are no real secrets in business—only truths you haven't yet figured out how to apply. This book will help you move these truths into the realm of execution— the place where innovation and action come together to make growth happen.

But first, a tiny physiology lesson. Want to know why referral generation is one of most effective yet elusive forms of marketing?

There is a tiny part of the brain, the hypothalamus, that—among other things—helps regulate sexual urges, thirst and hunger, maternal behavior, aggression, pleasure, and, to some degree, your propensity to refer.

The hypothalamus likes validation—it registers pleasure in doing good and being recognized for it, and it's home to the need to belong to something greater than ourselves. This is the social drive for making referrals.

Human beings are physiologically wired to make referrals. That's why so many businesses can grow and thrive by tapping this business-building strategy alone.

Reality #1: People make referrals because they need to

If you're one of those people who feels a bit shy about focusing on, let alone actually asking for, referrals, then the first thing you need to understand is this:

We rate and refer as a form of survival. Think about it. What happens when someone asks you for a good tailor? If you know one, you spill; if you don't, you think about it and maybe make a call or two. Instinctively, we know we are going to need a good tip someday, so we pass on what we know to others to build credit in the community. I imagine the roots of this notion go back to a time when relying on a good hunting or fishing tip may have meant the difference between life and death.

We refer to connect with other people. Being recognized as a source of good information, including referrals, is a great way to connect with others. Think about how eagerly you responded the last time someone asked you for directions, offering up your favorite shortcut and tips for avoiding traffic. We all do it. Making referrals is a deeply satisfying way to connect with others—asking for referrals is just the other side of the same phenomenon. I think the growth of many popular social networks can be traced to the fact that people love to connect and form communities around shared ideas.

I asked some people in one of my business networks to tell me about some of their favorite businesses. Seattle business coach Tammy Redmon's (www.tammyredmon.com) response illustrates this point nicely: "One of our favorite destination points is Voodoo Doughnuts (www.voodoodoughnut.com). It is an incredible little hole-in-the-wall on Third and Burnside in Portland, Oregon, with room inside the door for about eight to ten people. Their signature Voodoo Doughnut is out of this world, and the creativity they put into each creation is awe inspiring. It doesn't matter if you like donuts or not, you must go for the experience.

It is not to be missed when in Portland. Just plan on waiting in line; each time I have gone the line has been thirty-plus deep around the block. No kidding! 'The magic is in the hole!'"

We refer to build our own form of social currency. Providing a referral is a little like making a deposit. There is a natural law most humans ascribe to: If you do something for me, I am implicitly obligated to do something for you. Building up large stores of social capital is what makes some folks tick. This thinking is what drives some to become human databases. Their "go to" status when someone needs a referral is a carefully crafted asset. But understand that the laws of social currency and financial currency don't operate in the same manner. Social-currency building comes from a place of help rather than gain. Building social currency doesn't involve any strict form of accounting—the universe seems to sort that out with a give-to-get mentality.

Reality #2: All business involves risk

Unfortunately, a small but very distinct region of the hypothalamus also monitors, controls, and analyzes that powerful emotion known as fear. We constantly balance and measure, often at subconscious levels, pleasure and fear, gain and pain, and every action's likelihood to produce one or the other.

While we are indeed wired to give referrals, they also represent a potential risk. When we make a referral, we are putting the trust we have established with the recipient on loan to the person or company being referred.

Of course, risk varies in degree according to the magnitude of the referred party's need. There is more risk in referring a friend to, for instance, a good accountant, than in referring one to a place for authentic Thai. But as we dive into the strategies and tactics of some real-world referable businesses you'll see that a trust-building approach to marketing reduces fear and risk for a referrer in any scenario.

The surest way to remove risk is to build a business or product that connects with customers on both logical and emotional levels.

Or, as Fred Reichheld, author of *The Ultimate Question* puts it—head and heart.

People make decisions about the businesses they refer the same way they make decisions about a purchase. We simultaneously weigh whether something is affordable, fits well, or addresses a need—the head part—and whether we will look good, feel smart, or enjoy ourselves—the heart part. If the emotional pull is very strong, you can rationalize away what may otherwise stand out as a logical shortcoming, like a steep price.

Most businesses focus on the logical elements—price, features and benefits, a desired result—while ignoring the emotional rewards that are essential for the total customer experience.

People don't get emotional and passionate about ordinary products, a satisfactory result, or a fair price. They talk about things that surprise them or make them feel great about themselves—and, in effect, remove the feeling of risk they might have about doing business with that firm.

It's not enough to have a good solution. Buzzed-about businesses have a good solution draped in a total experience that excites, delights, or surprises the customer and motivates them to voluntarily talk about their experience.

Nona Jordan (Biznik.com/members/nona-jordan), a life coach and yoga instructor in Italy, related this story to me about a surprising experience she had: "I ordered a singing bowl from Fabeku before vacation. During vacation, I checked my e-mail to discover a really wonderful e-mail thank-you from him, telling me that he had sent the bowl. In addition to that, he also complimented my Web site and said some things which indicated he actually took a look around, which made my day.

"Even more impressive, when I picked up the package today, I ripped into it in the parking lot, unable to wait to see the bowl. Imagine my surprise, and utter delight, when the first thing I saw was a handwritten card! Digging through the little white packing kernels excitedly, I then found a package of incense! Brilliant! *Then*, just to make it even more amazing, the bowl was wrapped like a gift, and really, I still can't stop grinning."

Reality #3: Nobody talks about boring businesses

I interviewed marketing philosopher extraordinaire Seth Godin, author of books such as *Purple Cow* and *The Dip*, for an episode of the *Duct Tape Marketing* podcast. We talked about referrals and word of mouth and, in typical Seth fashion, he shared this profound nugget.

"If the marketplace isn't talking about you," he said, "there's a reason. The reason is that you're boring. And you're probably boring on purpose. You have boring pricing because that's safer. You have a boring location because to do otherwise would be nuts. You have boring products because that's what the market wants."

Author and speaker Scott Ginsberg gets talked about—all the time.

Encountering Ginsberg in a crowded room, you would most likely find him to be an unassuming, polite, energetic, nice guy. He's probably wearing faded jeans, sandals, and sporting that intentionally unkempt hairstyle common with the twenty-something set these days. At first blush there's nothing extraordinary about Ginsberg, except that everywhere he goes people approach him.

At the diner, in the airport, at a meeting, standing in line at the coffee shop, on the bus—it's always the same. It starts with a look, then perhaps a whisper to a friend in a cupped hand, and finally people are drawn to approach Ginsberg and say something like: "Dude, you're wearing a name tag."

And sure enough, there it is right on his coat—"Hello, my name is Scott." The conversation begins.

Scott Ginsberg has made a business out of doing essentially one thing—wearing a name tag every single day, all day, for, at the time of this writing, over eight years.

The way Ginsberg tells it, he went to a social event in college where attendees were asked to wear name tags. Afterward, he went about his business but forgot to remove his name tag. (We've all done that, right?)

What Ginsberg found was that his name tag made him more approachable. Wearing it, he stood out and got attention. So he decided to keep wearing it, and made the wearing of a name tag his core personal branding element.

Today, Ginsberg speaks to thousands of businesses and individuals on the subject of approachability, a subject he's also written eight books about. Ginsberg is very, very good at what he does, and that's why people keep hiring him. But Ginsberg's secret referral weapon is that people can't help talking about his commitment to wearing a name tag every day for the rest of his life. It's simply remarkable.

To build a business, territory, or practice based primarily on referrals, you must first discover or create the remarkable thing about you or your products, the thing that gets people talking, that almost forces them to tell others about you. Boring people, products, and companies are hard to refer!

Ginsberg is highly referable because he's found a way to clearly differentiate himself from his competitors. People can't help talking about him.

Reality #4: Consistency builds trust

In his presentations, Scott Ginsberg often recounts stories of people being so threatened by his name tag that they actually wanted to fight him. He tells of people hurling insults at him, ripping the tag from his coat—he's even received e-mailed death threats for his tag-wearing ways! (People obviously not getting enough ketchup in their diets.)

Next time you see Ginsberg, I invite you to (gently) peel the name tag from his topcoat; it's okay, he's got one on his blazer, and another on his shirt. And just in case your group needs him to present at your next pool party, he's got his name tag permanently tattooed on his chest. So yeah, he's committed to his brand and to his primary referral strategy.

What Ginsberg adds to this equation is an unquestionable commitment to his differentiation, his consistent talkability factor.

It does very little good to create this week's publicity stunt in an effort to get folks talking for today. Referability is a long-term game;

it's not a drive-by event but a well-planned, precisely calculated marathon. Repetition, consistency, and authenticity build trust and are the foundational tools of the referral trade. People can sense when you are attempting to draw attention for attention's sake, or are stepping out of your authentic self so far that it doesn't feel right to you or anyone associated with your business.

Commitment to a remarkable difference demonstrates that yours is not a gimmick.

Reality #5: Marketing is a system

At the core, a fully functioning business is basically a set of systems and processes. Marketing is a system, finance is a system, and management is a system. If you follow this line of thinking, then referral generation is a set of processes within the overall marketing system. And yet, the most common objections I hear when I suggest implementing a systematic approach to generating referrals—I don't deserve referrals, I feel funny asking for referrals, my parents told me it's not proper to beg for business—are other ways of saying, "I don't really have any idea why someone would want to talk about my business." These feel more like excuses steeped in self-doubt than reasons.

I've witnessed excuses like these melting under the bright light of a step-by-step referral generation system, one based on a complete understanding of the value you bring and that enlists the complete cooperation of customers and partners in bringing that value to others. You must embrace the true value your organization produces and develop a referral system that allows you to bring the best of your authentic self to every opportunity.

While some people may think of a "system" as a tool for process freaks to lean on, this book will show you how your referral system will be essential to holding yourself accountable for getting your head and your butt in gear.

Ivana Taylor runs a company called DIY Marketers, and by her own admission is painfully shy. Painfully shy and asking for referrals don't normally go hand in hand. Taylor did some strategic soul-searching and realized that asking a customer for a referral felt too personal, so she just didn't do it. Unfortunately, she had successfully targeted a narrow niche market and knew that her business would sink or swim based on her ability to get referrals from happy customers. There simply was no other form of marketing or advertising that would allow her to get her business in front of the key CEOs in her chosen area.

Taylor's solution was to take advantage of her years of experience in consulting with businesses on the creation of productivity processes. She established a set of processes that she could put on autopilot. Now, when a CEO became a client, they would begin to automatically receive a series of communications that subtly outlined her process of working by referral. When she let her processes do the asking, she began to feel less negative about asking for referrals—and potentially being rejected by a prospective customer—and consequently she got over her fear, asked consistently for referrals, and dramatically increased the number of referrals and customers she started to receive.

Many people I encounter get tripped up over this same idea. Your belief that asking for referrals is like begging for business is a personal problem. One of the ways to get the "you" out of the way is through a system that energizes others to voluntarily promote you and your products for their own reasons.

But if you don't feel strongly enough about the value you or your products deliver to expect that your clients will voluntarily make an effort to see that others receive it, then there is little chance that you will ever come to depend on a consistent flow of referrals. Expecting referrals is not about you; it's about getting the customer what's possible. Find a way to detach yourself from any personal feelings of pride or self-doubt and get to work on creating a brilliant system that's focused on getting results for your customers.

Here's the really magical thing: For Taylor, overcoming her personal fear of asking for referrals through the use of a system allowed her to be more authentic and available for her clients. A major component of her referral system was the formation of roundtables that brought her customers together to network and build referrals among each other.

So don't get tripped up on the system concept. As we move to design and implement your total referral system you'll discover that there is no one system that works for everyone. In fact, that's the shortcoming of much of what's taught on the subject of referrals: Experts try to cram everyone into the same box and the same set of steps for generating referrals.

Maybe you've tried to develop some referral or networking techniques, only to discover that they either didn't work for you or you didn't work for them—either way, eventually you may have simply given up on the notion.

In this book we will present a framework—beginning with the set-up of realities addressed in this chapter—a set of overarching strategies, high- and low-tech engagement tools, and a methodology for finding your perfect culture of referral. We will also provide a host of specific tactical examples in an effort to help you design the only system that will bring you the results you desire, because it's the only referral system designed by and for you and no one else.

In fact, the ideal referral system, based on a strategy that gets people voluntarily talking about your business, can eliminate the need to ever actually ask for referrals again.

The most tragic referral reality

Before we move on, I want to share something that I find astonishing about this referral business. In preparation for writing this book, I conducted an informal survey of several thousand small business owners. Unsurprisingly, I found that 63.4 percent felt that over half their business came by way of referrals. But of that same group, 79.9 percent readily admitted that they had no system of any kind to generate referrals.

This is somewhat puzzling. How can a business owner know that word of mouth is so powerful and then do so little to take advantage of it?

Consider this direct response from a survey participant, and the plight of what I like to call the accidental referral becomes a little easier to frame and dissect:

> We have trouble getting and asking for referrals from our customers. When we ask they say, "I'll keep it in mind." When we try to offer an incentive, we still get nothing. Because of that, we just don't ask! I would think getting referrals from happy customers would be easier!

In this survey, participants were asked what gets in the way of generating referrals. The answers included "fear," "desperation," and "don't think to ask," to name a few, but, in the end, the real reason is a multi-layered portrayal of the most tragic business reality of all.

You know how powerful referral can be, but you're not doing anything worth being talked about. Or, if you are, you lack an authentic and systematic approach to stimulating conversations, collecting leads, educating prospects, and converting those referrals into customers.

CHAPTER 2

The Qualities of Referral

I have had the opportunity to discuss business and marketing strategies with hundreds of business owners. I am fascinated by how often successful, referral-generating businesses cited the same elements and practices as the secret to their success. In some cases these were intentional, and in others it was a matter of a business acting authentically and practicing what felt right intuitively only to discover the marketing value later.

While the qualities of a referable business I have identified through my interviews and observations may not come naturally to all, they can be learned and instilled in any business with enough effort.

The most trusted option

In the business of referrals, trust is the most important reason a recommendation is made and, conversely, lack of trust the single greatest reason referrals don't happen. There are countless ways that companies build and break trust with their customers, but most can be summed up with the term "honesty."

Janine Popick, CEO of Vertical Response, a San Francisco–based *Inc.* 500 e-mail marketing service, recounted this story from the very early days of her business. As a start-up she had very few customers, let alone very few big-name customers. So keeping the e-mail market-ing business of ACT! Software was significant. ACT! depended heav-ily on its e-mail campaigns to prospect and keep customers up-to-date with upgrades and training. Vertical Response's servers had been expe-riencing technical issues, and Popick worried about her company's abil-ity to continue to make ACT! look good if e-mail delivery was spotty or sent incorrectly.

Rather than crossing her fingers and hoping all went well, Popick went to the marketing director at ACT! and asked to be fired. She explained the technical issues they were experiencing and suggested that another company might be more reliable at this point. Her cus-tomer was so impressed with Popick's honesty that they remained a customer and a passionate voice of referrals for Vertical Response for many years.

"I think more than anything it's about meeting people's expecta-tions," Popick told me. "If something goes wrong we tell them what to expect, do exactly what we promise to fix it, and communicate fully throughout the process. That's what we've always tried to do."

Trust is earned by keeping promises: tangible things like delivering on time, paying bills on time, and honoring guarantees; and less tangi-ble things like authentic marketing messages, caring service, and a cul-ture of respect.

Trust is also lost by overpromising. I'm not suggesting that you shouldn't aim high, but I am suggesting you must know what you are capable of doing and do what you say you are going to do. It sounds so simple, yet it's the number one reason people lose faith in businesses and in entire industries.

When you have trust—earned by keeping your promises—you can make mistakes, own up to them, and correct them without loss. One of the hallmarks of a highly referred business is that they work as hard on fixing mistakes as on any other aspect of their business.

Of course, there are two sides to trust. Trust is a quality that must be extended as well as earned. You can see this in the types of employ-ees an organization attracts and develops by trusting their staff to make smart, customer-focused decisions.

The importance of trust as a referral currency is somewhat dependent on the importance/risk a purchaser places on the purchase—either in terms of human cost or actual cost. The higher the price tag, the more essential the service, the more vital trust becomes to the relationship. But even a company selling a twenty-nine-dollar-a-month service will live and die over time based on the level of trust it builds with its customers, employees, and partners.

I receive offers for cheap Web hosting almost daily. While the cost of the service in question is almost insignificant, the cost of having my site off-line or hacked could be catastrophic. I choose my service very carefully and put a great deal of stock in the recommendations of others I trust, even though it's a relatively low-cost item.

Think about your own experience. When was the last time you referred a friend to a business you kind of trusted? Show me a business that automatically receives a substantial amount of business by way of referral and, with rare exception, you'll find a business that places supreme value on building and keeping trust in every aspect of business.

It's possible to build a business or product that people simply love to talk about, even though it's not always trustworthy. But these are few and far between, and often owe more to quirks in popular culture than a sustainable business plan.

Stephen Covey, author of *The SPEED of Trust*, put it in even more tangible terms when I asked him to explain his concept of trust as it relates to speed. "Trust," he stated, "always impacts speed and cost. When you have high trust everything can move faster and costs less, it's like creating a trust investment; of course, the opposite is true of a low-trust environment, or a kind trust tax. This is what makes trust more than a nice social asset; it's a hard-edge business asset as well."

Staff as customer

Here's something your customers won't ever tell you but that you had better understand: Your employees probably treat your customers about the same way you treat your employees. Let that soak that in for a minute, and think about the ways your everyday behavior might be affecting your organization's ability to generate referrals.

Organizations that easily generate a high number of referrals consider referral factors when they hire and treat their employees like prime target customers. It makes sense, of course; happy employees are much more likely to represent the brand in a positive manner. Let's face it: Companies aren't capable of making emotional connections; people are. But it takes effort.

In all but the most technical positions, much of what employees do on a day-to-day basis can be taught. It's much harder, however, to teach someone to be trustworthy, to give, or to serve. Yet, as stated above, these are key traits of organizations that generate referrals. If your organization has more than two or three employees it's a pretty good bet they will interact with customers and prospects in ways that will affect your brand. So the question is, are you hiring and training to create a referral culture?

It's become almost cliché to write about the online shoe retailer Zappos (www.zappos.com) when covering the topic of referrals and word of mouth. After all, much of the company's meteoric rise came about through the buzz of passionate customers, and it's a story people love to share.

Sometimes, however, we read about what great customer service a company has and we fail to credit the innovative processes and hard work that went into creating it. Zappos forged an incredible culture-building tool it calls "The Offer." Most Zappos employees work the phones in customer service roles. When a new employee joins Zappos, they go through four weeks of paid training and are immersed in the company's strategy, culture, and obsession with customers.

About a week into the process Zappos makes "The Offer." They tell each employee that, if they quit that day, they will be paid for the week of work plus $1,000 to quit. What Zappos discovered was that if someone was willing to take them up on the offer, then it probably means they were never going to be the kind of customer-obsessed, high-energy employee so important to the brand. At one point I read that less than 10 percent of new employees take the money and quit. My guess is that the cost of keeping uncommitted folks far exceeds the offer cost in letting them go.

Hire for fit

One recurring thread in many of the businesses I interviewed was the idea of hiring the right people. And this notion starts first with knowing who or what that is. In much the same way a business might research and attempt to attract the ideal customer, referral-based businesses also focus on attracting the ideal employee.

The company takes care of the staff, the staff takes care of the customer, the customer takes care of the business.

Southwest Airlines is famous for their service. They openly admit they "hire for attitude, and train for skill." One of the ways they hire for attitude is through a thorough and somewhat offbeat interview process.

Part of the process requires applicants to fill out and read aloud a personal "Coat of Arms"—a questionnaire on which applicants complete statements such as: "One time my sense of humor helped me was"; "A time I reached my peak performance was"; and "My personal motto is."

Applicants are often put into groups and given a group task aimed at sorting out attitudes and leadership qualities.

Many Southwest employees have their own hiring stories; Scott Kirk, a Southwest pilot, shared on the company's blog that he even used his "celebrity" name (Captain Kirk of TV's *Star Trek*) to help him get the job at Southwest. "When I first applied for a pilot position at Southwest, I sent a photograph of one of the Boeing 737 aircrafts painted as the USS *Enterprise*," said Scott. "At the bottom of the photo I wrote, 'Hey Herb, beam me aboard will ya?' I was shocked when I received a personal letter from Mr. Kelleher himself wishing me luck in the interview and warm wishes to hopefully beam me aboard soon. From that moment on, I knew that I had chosen the right airline."

Mike McDerment, founder of FreshBooks (www.freshbooks.com), an online time-tracking and invoicing service located in Toronto, Canada, shared these thoughts on how he addresses the customer-employee relationship: "First, we try to find people for fit, shared values, and a passion for excellence. That doesn't mean we have some preconceived idea of what they look like. It's more that they match our brand in some way. We're not in the billing business, we're in the service business, and we like to have fun. It really makes things easy if we surround our customers with employees that like to serve and like to have fun as well."

FreshBooks also encourages internal innovation by hosting biweekly opportunities for its software developers to contribute to the company through something they call "Hack-Offs." In a nutshell, a hack-off is a day of unstructured time for developers to work on any project they like. "Sometimes it's improvements to the product," McDerment explained. "Things nagging customers but that we just haven't gotten to. Sometimes it's things nagging the developers that they just want to fix and no one else will see. And other times it's a proof of concept of some new technology. The only guiding rule about what to work on is that they should be able to finish it in a day."

Whatever they are working on throughout the day, at 4:30 P.M. the developers stop. At that point, the entire company moves through the office, from screen to screen, and gets demos from each developer on what they've created. Once all the demos are done, they vote for their favorite. Beyond peer recognition, the company usually bestows movie tickets or Raptors basketball tickets on the winner.

This brilliant tactic is a highlight of the workweek and puts the focus on innovation and constant improvement of the product and service experience. In doing so, it turns work into a game, a game with a few simple rules and a clear way to win.

Train, and create standards

The second element of the staff as customer involves training. Regular, institutionalized training is a core element of widely referred businesses. This begins with training in the daily routines and processes required to complete ordinary job functions, but it goes much deeper as well.

Sarah Endline, CEO of sweetriot (www.sweetriot.com), a maker of specialty dark chocolate candy located in New York City, devotes a large portion of its "riotation"—her company's term for orientation—on teaching the company mission and culture, and the history of the company, the industry, and the product category, before ever diving into how to fulfill and ship an order.

Teaching every new employee everything you can about your organization's marketing strategy, marketing plan, positioning, messaging, ideal customer, products, services, and brand attributes just makes sense when it comes to creating ambassadors of the organization. Consistently providing marketing training for the entire staff is one key to getting everyone involved in generating referrals.

Often it's your staff that owns the frontline customer, partner, and prospect relationship. Smart companies makes sure every employee understands how to spot an ideal customer, how to properly introduce the company's story, and how to spot trigger phrases prospective customers use, and clues they give, that mark them as potential ideal customers, even if selling isn't a part of that employee's job description.

This basic training should be implemented at the outset and consistently and repeatedly reinforced.

Give them the tools

Another element of the employee-as-customer habit lies in the word "empowerment." While the word empowerment shows up in almost every book ever written about management, it's a term that is easy to say but not so easy to put into action.

In their 1999 book, *First, Break All the Rules: What the World's Greatest Managers Do Differently*, Marcus Buckingham and Curt Coffman published findings from research conducted by the Gallup Organization involving eighty thousand managers across different industries. They used this research to conclude that if a company can't satisfy an employee's basic needs first, it can never expect that employee to deliver stellar performance. The research indicated that a productive employee's basic needs are: knowing what is expected at work; having the equipment and support to do the work right; and receiving appropriate praise and feedback for work accomplished.

Referred companies place so much focus on delighting customers that employees grow to understand that the primary thing that is expected, and even measured, about their performance is the generation of referrals from customers.

When this expectation is then reinforced with tools that put the focus on the outcome as much as on the process, they often learn to do whatever it takes to get a positive result. Positive reinforcement follows. This is one of the hardest adjustments a small business owner can make as the business grows.

Larry Ryan founded Ryan Lawn and Tree (www.ryanlawn.com) over twenty years ago. He started out on the backseat of a tractor and grew the business steadily by taking care of his customers and employees. Today he is the CEO of one of the largest lawn-care services in the Midwest, with over 150 employees. "The hardest job I have," he admits, "is getting out of the way and letting my people do what they need to do."

Ryan has always run his business with the philosophy that every customer should be thrilled, and that no matter how illogical the customer's demand, he would try to satisfy it. This philosophy has caused him to scratch his head in disbelief at times, but Ryan can also relate countless instances when thrilled customers have written him notes about, for instance, a turf manager coming back on his own accord to redo a patch of grass that just didn't work out right the first time.

Ryan hires for organizational fit and talent, and his employees are clear on what is expected of them and are given the tools, permission, and encouragement to take matters into their own hands to achieve the ultimate objective of customer satisfaction. As a result, his business, generated primarily through referrals, has grown steadily year in and year out for over twenty years.

Open dashboard

Another common trait among staff-oriented businesses is an openness to communicating the financial aspects of the business. For instance, sweetriot offers stock ownership to its employees as a way to keep everyone focused on the growth of the company.

Creating a "dashboard," a simple one-page, high-level view of key strategic, marketing, and financial indicators allows even those in entry-level positions to be a part of the company's success and strategic vision. It's also a great way to keep everyone in the organization focused on key goals like referral generation.

New Belgium Brewing Company (www.newbelgium.com), based in Fort Collins, Colorado, was named one of fifteen "Top Small Work-places" in the United States by the *Wall Street Journal* in 2008. A brief tour of the place provides a glimpse into why. (And no, I'm not referring to the unlimited supply of Fat Tire Amber Ale.) New Belgium's staff is made up of owners, and it shows in the pride and enthusiasm demon-strated through every contact, from the phone to the tasting room.

New Belgium began operations in a Fort Collins basement in 1991. Today they are the third-largest craft brewer in the United States. At the time of the *WSJ* award, New Belgium boasted a 97 percent employee retention rate and practiced a full-disclosure financial reporting system often referred to as "open book management." And at the end of one year of employment, a staff member becomes an owner.

This note from the company's Web site speaks to the culture of ownership at New Belgium: "Employees are guided by this simple prin-ciple: If it were your company, what would you do? Look for ways to be less wasteful, be more efficient, recycle, and reuse? Yep. It's infec-tious. Once you start thinking of ways to make your company better, you can't stop."

New Belgium CEO Kim Jordan explains their open-book philosophy like this: "The way it works here is that each employee knows precisely what it costs to make a barrel of beer, and how much their department contributes to that cost. Since they have a vested interest in the profits, they often meet to set performance targets to bring those costs down. They determine which costs trouble them—keep them up at night—and then they recommend how they can do better. We're proud of the corporate culture we've established here. Our employees care—about the product, about costs, and about each other. It's not unusual for an employee to stay late to help a coworker get a certain job done."

Employee as owner

In March 1982 Paul Saginaw and Ari Weinzweig opened Zingerman's Deli (www.zingermans.com) in a historic building near the Ann Arbor Farmers' Market. Today Zingerman's is an Ann Arbor, Michigan, institution, the source of great food and great experiences for tens of thousands of visitors every year. *Inc.* magazine called Zingerman's the "coolest company in America," and when Ari and Paul made an appearance on *Oprah*, she rated their sandwiches an 11 out of 5.

I had an opportunity to visit with Weinzweig, and I discovered that not only does the business serve up great sandwiches, they have a great story as well. Zingerman's grew so popular that franchising nationwide seemed inevitable. However, the owners chose another path. Instead of growing the deli business beyond where they wanted to go, they started other businesses around their single store. Today they run a mail-order business (look for the chocolate-covered bacon), a catering business, a coffee-roasting business, and a bake house. ZingTrain, perhaps their most unique offshoot, shares the company's expertise in training, service, merchandising, specialty foods, and staff management with other businesses through seminars and one-on-one consulting.

One unique aspect of the model is that all the businesses are started by managing partners who own a share of the business. The umbrella business is Zingerman's Community of Businesses (www.zingermanscommunity.com). Anyone is free to come to Zingerman's with an idea for a business and pitch it as a candidate to join the community. Several of the existing businesses were launched by Zingerman's employees.

Does it work? According to Weinzweig, the Zingerman's experience is now made and delivered by nearly five hundred people—partners, managers, and staff in six different businesses in addition to the deli—to the tune of roughly $36 million in annual sales.

The fun and friendly nature of this business is a big part of what gets people buzzing. I think it's best summed up by Weinzweig through a sentiment he shared during an NPR *Weekend Edition* interview: "Fun is in our guiding principles and it's in the 2020 Vision. Life is short, and even when times are hard, which they have been and I'm sure will be again, it's important to enjoy the people and the food and the customers and everything that we get to be around them. I mean, I feel very fortunate to be around such a great group of people and to work with such great products."

A culture of buzz

Highly referred businesses are good enough to make people want to talk about them, but they amplify this natural desire by making word of mouth an essential element of the culture. Companies create buzz with great follow-up, T-shirts and other promotional merchandise, free events, outrageous acts of kindness—anything that contributes to an overall culture of buzz.

Mike McDerment shared a great example of this kind of buzz thinking at FreshBooks with me. He had written a post on the company blog about his love for Triscuit crackers and their tasty new flavors. (Simply sharing this kind of personal story with customers is one element of the FreshBooks culture of buzz.) One of his customers wrote a tongue-in-cheek response asking that they not talk about Triscuits because he could not get them where he lived—in Fiji: "I'd like to request removal from all future postings which reference food items I'm unable to purchase in this country. I am right now dying to try cracked pepper and olive oil Triscuits. I am seriously considering cancelling my FreshBooks [sic] account because of this irresponsible posting. Have a heart—Jonathan."

So what did Mike and company do? They ran out and purchased some boxes of cracked pepper and olive oil Triscuits and shipped them off to Jonathan in Fiji. Then they had a good laugh and went back to work.

Well, some eight thousand miles away, their thrilled customer was busy blogging about the incredible thing his billing-software service had done.

I'm tempted to go on and on about the social implications of people just doing nice things for the sake of doing them, but I'll refrain from that and simply write: FreshBooks, you've got a customer for a life and yet one more person to sing your praises to the masses.

This story of going the extra mile was picked up all over the Internet, and FreshBooks benefitted from a ministorm of positive buzz. Like most viral buzz hits, Mike's act began as a spontaneous act of inspired customer service rather than any kind of calculated attempt to garner publicity—and that's precisely why it was so effective.

Companies that focus on creating positive customer experiences at every turn tap the power of buzz quite naturally, and this habit is something that can be learned. Let me emphasize the natural and authentic nature of this habit. A culture of buzz is not created by attempting to do things that get attention; customers recognize publicity stunts when they see them.

The most effective long-term cultural shift for most organizations comes when the focus is put on making the total customer experience something worth talking about on a case-by-case basis. Every now and then you get a nice little bonus of some great PR or word-of-mouth buzz, but it all starts with one customer thinking to themselves: "Wow, that was kinda cool."

Today's Web technology makes it very easy to create buzz online as well as to encourage your customers to generate ratings, reviews, and other content about your products and services.

Give-to-get mentality

There are a handful of golden rules, which vary depending on which set of books you were raised on, but in the business of referrals, those who give usually get.

It's not too hard to grasp this concept; everyone in business has experienced the "what goes around comes around" phenomenon. But I'd like to suggest that something deeper exists in the true referral-based mind-set. When a referral strategy pervades your entire business thinking, you begin to approach customer relationships by asking "What am I here to give?" or "How can I serve?" as opposed to "What can I sell?" You begin to look for and develop strategic partner relationships with a view toward adding value to your existing customer relationships instead of as a means to get in front of new prospects. Developing this perspective can change the entire architecture of your organization and transform the effectiveness of your marketing efforts.

For some successful referral generators, this way of thinking is the primary driving force of their business relationships. Dixie Gillaspie, a business coach located in the Midwest, has built a substantial reputation as someone who connects people, and looks for ways to grow her business by giving leads and introductions to help those in her network get what they are looking for. "Your network is your safety net and your fishing net," she explained to me. "It will save your life and feed you for life if you build it well and treat it right."

Dixie is a die-hard networker, and has even created a coaching program based on the bestselling book *The Go-Giver* by Bob Burg and John David Mann. In *The Go-Giver*, we meet an ambitious young man named Joe, who is introduced to the Five Laws of Stratospheric Success.

Joe learns that changing his focus from getting to giving—putting others' interests first and continually adding value to their lives—ultimately leads to unexpected returns. The Law of Value states: "Your true worth is determined by how much more you give in value than you take in payment." The Law of Compensation states: "Your income is determined by how many people you serve and how well you serve them."

"In the last five years," Gillaspie said, "I've only worked with two clients who did not come to me as a result of networking. Referrals have been from networking connections and from clients who were originally referred by networking connections." As we move on to developing your referral system, you can bet I will introduce you to many ways to build a solid give-to-get network.

Expect referrals

It stands to reason that a customer who comes to your organization by way of referral and then experiences your remarkable level of service is far more likely to become part of your referral team. Remarkable companies expect to receive referrals as a matter of course. In fact, they are confident something went wrong with their process when a customer does not voluntarily refer.

Now, I get some pushback when I wander too near this idea of expecting referrals. So I'm going to push you a little here. If you truly believe that your products and services offer world-class solutions, then you are doing your customers a disservice by not making it very easy for them to introduce these benefits to their friends.

If you find yourself saying, "I believe you get referrals by doing good work, not by asking for them," then I'm going to suggest that you're not really sure of the value of your products and services. Remarkable companies always ask for referrals, not simply as a way to acquire new business, but also as a way to help the most people get the results they are after.

This is not an arrogant point of view. When you come to believe in—without question—the value you can deliver, then making that value available to as many people as possible becomes the higher purpose of your business.

This is where your authentic referral system will serve you most. When you are clear about your company's value and build a systematic culture of referral, you can come to expect referrals that are both authentic and profitable.

Premium pricing

Too often price is the first and only measure of differentiation when a prospect attempts to compare products, services, and organizations. In the eyes of a prospect, there is risk involved in any transaction no matter how large or small. So, the prospect thinks, if it doesn't work out with the low-priced company, at least I didn't overpay.

Referred prospects, on the other hand, have the ability to factor value into the equation. When your business comes highly recommended by a friend, the role of risk is minimized, and that fact alone moves the significance of price comparison down the list.

In fact, when introduced to a company by a friend as the best possible choice, prospects often anticipate paying a premium for your products or services, and do so willingly once some measure of social proof has been factored in.

I have yet to find a business that relies heavily on referrals and low-price leadership as shared strategies. Remarkable businesses generally lie on the upper end of the industry norm when it comes to pricing. The supplement to this habit is that widely referred businesses also invest in their people and are rarely the low-wage leader in the industry either.

Larry Ryan of Ryan Lawn and Tree readily admits that they compete by adding employees looking for a career instead of a part-time job. Most of Ryan's lawn-care specialists possess degrees and training in the field of horticulture. This in an industry that commonly offers only part-time, hourly wages to anyone willing to do the manual labor involved in caring for lawns and trees.

The impact of this idea on a firm's profit is reason enough to focus every ounce of your organization's marketing muscle on referral generation as the preferred method of introduction to prospective customers. Every widely referred business I interviewed was one of the highest priced options in their respective markets and felt no pressure to compete on price.

Inbound versus outbound

Many widely referred business do very little when it comes to traditional advertising and lead generation; word on the street, happy customers, and actively engaged partners account for a great deal of their efforts. This has tremendous implications when it comes to marketing budgets. One of the single greatest marketing expenses for a business is paid advertising placement.

In the traditional, outbound form of lead generation involving a "broadcast your sales message and then go hunt for customers" approach, there is a built-in wall of resistance that prospects use to protect themselves from being sold on something by a salesperson or ad. Businesses focused on generating referrals turn their attention to education over selling, in an effort to teach or demonstrate that they have what the prospect needs. Add to this dynamic the fact that the prospect may have already actually witnessed the results your products or services brought to their friends and colleagues, and you have one highly likely lead.

When a referral occurs it is often because someone has expressed a very specific need or challenge and your firm has been offered as a solution by a trustworthy person. That's why I refer to this as inbound lead generation. Leads aren't sold to; they decide to buy.

Not long ago I was asked by a large insurance carrier to help design a marketing system for their new agents. They had been using the same technique for about fifty years. It went like this. Every new agent would make up a list of a hundred people they knew, from friends to relatives to professional connections. Next, they would get on the phone and ask those people, some of whom they hadn't seen them in years, to consider working with this insurance newbie on taking care of the needs of their family and property. Once that list was exhausted, their next option was to start pounding the phones, in the equally frustrating game of cold calling.

Scary thing is, this is pretty much the approach of 90 percent of the companies in this industry. In fact, this is a common approach for all too many businesses. But outbound marketing, interrupting anyone with a pulse, or, worse yet, a family member who might actually buy out of guilt is a thing of the past.

My advice for this company was this: Have your new agents make that same list. But instead of pitching them on insurance, introduce them to other businesses, services, and opportunities. In fact, I suggested that they spend the first six months of this new program doing nothing but connecting their friends, family, and network members in ways that helped them get more of what they were lacking—no selling allowed.

It may feel counterintuitive, I explained to my client, to put the sales approach on the back burner and focus simply on making referrals, but do it and people will find you—that's the essence of the inbound referral.

They fired me.

Shorter sales cycle

The phone rings one Tuesday morning and an excited prospect on the other end of the line wants to know when you can come out and start work on their project. Seems they got your name from Chuck, who said you basically saved his life. "Oh, and do you accept credit cards?"

My hope is that you've experienced that kind of "sales" call at some point. It's pretty nice when it happens, isn't it? But that's another advantage of the referral-based business. When a prospect has been presold by a happy customer, the process of making a deal and deciding on a price is often a pretty short one.

Widely referred businesses still have lead-qualification and -conversion processes; you still need to make sure that Chuck explained how you work, who you work with, and the unique value your firm can bring before actually taking the order. But that process can occur more quickly when your prospect's natural sales resistance has been lowered by the referral.

Ahmed Mady, founder of Paragon Remodeling (www.paragonre modeling.com) in Virginia, takes it a step further. He has a process to qualify every lead that comes by way of referral. But instead of turning away referred leads that are not a good fit for his business, he treats the leads just like a customer and helps them get what they need from another source. While this practice doesn't always net him any immediate revenue, he finds that it often leads to an introduction to other work that is a fit from the referred business, as well as referrals from a prospect thrilled they could find the right company to complete their project.

Process oriented

Companies that rely on referrals, on creating remarkable experiences for their customers, are generally more system-oriented.

Again from Mady of Paragon Remodeling: "We employ technology that allows our customers and prospects to get in touch with and set appointments with our project managers in real time. We confirm every appointment. This ease of contact and professional process alone nets us referrals."

By creating processes to deliver consistent experiences, Paragon builds trust, empowers their employees to achieve results, and creates paths for successful growth. It's pretty simple to manage the customer experience when it's you and Louie taking the calls. When your business grows, you must replace your successful habits with successful systems in order to continue to deliver the highest level of service.

FreshBooks requires that every employee serve the customer at the most basic level. No matter what position someone is hired for, they spend time in customer support. Even the most senior staff members train initially in customer support and routinely take customer service and training calls.

"First you learn the product, then you learn the customer, and through that you learn the culture," FreshBooks founder Mike McDerment explained.

The secret to the success of this habit, according to McDerment, is the company's ability to walk the fine line of systems growth and systems choking. A system can create a negative customer experience if the person operating it doesn't have the flexibility to make decisions on the fly that are obviously in the best interest of the customer—even if they don't always follow the documented path. For FreshBooks, systems are a framework to deliver consistent results, but everyone knows what the ultimate goal is—wow the customer.

Proper processes and the building of a dynamic operations manual through collaboration tools such as wikis or an online project management tool such as Central Desktop (www.centraldesktop.com) is a great way to use technology to help plan for growth as well.

Every business, regardless of size, can benefit from the rich set of project management and collaboration tools available today. In fact, routinely documenting your processes is quite likely one of the most valuable practices you engage in.

Business owners often obsess over protecting assets, and rightly so. Assets are the tangible, hard-won elements that businesses use to help support a picture of overall health and value. But, let's expand the view of assets for a minute. Have you ever stopped to think about how valuable the collective knowledge of your business is worth? Aren't your success systems and processes, the "how we do it here" kinds of things, assets as well?

Many small businesses actually run, thrive, and grow based on figuring out how to do something better than everyone else in their industry, how to create a richer experience, how to deliver a better bang for the buck. To me, this knowledge is not only an asset, it's a crucial asset—well worth protecting.

Most employees, regardless of level of responsibility, do much better work when they understand what's expected and have a clear understanding of the routine work. In fact, a system that clearly shows how to get the desired result often frees people up to think about the more creative questions, such as: "How can we get the desired result faster?"

I've witnessed employees coming together in very positive ways around the idea of looking at every task a business does in strategic ways and linking how one job affects another and impacts the bottom line. All too often people toil away with very little appreciation for the effect their contribution has on the big picture. A knowledge and operations manual can help foster these kinds of connections internally.

By creating a simple tool and giving people the freedom to create and map the best processes for success, you may find that not only are you capturing valuable assets, you're empowering people to improve the assets.

That which makes you better

Let me end this chapter by getting some additional leverage. Simply adopting a referral mind-set and a number of the qualities described in this chapter can help you build a stronger business.

I've seen companies go through fundamental transitions simply by instituting the referral strategy and culture outlined in this book as an overall business strategy. If your plan is to set the referral threshold in your new marketing strategy at 100 percent—in other words, all of your customers are going to be so thrilled they will voluntarily refer others and voluntarily talk about your business—then things will need tightening up.

If you are going to explore ways to get your customers, partners, and staff to voluntarily and authentically talk about how remarkable your business is, just in that act alone, and the eventual changes it will require you to make will improve your business, if only because you've taken another look at ways you can be remarkable.

The outpouring of new energy this process produces means that you get better—in fact, you really have no choice. Your products get better, your service gets better, your follow-up gets better, your delivery gets better, your staff gets better, your ideas get better, your innovation gets better, your marketing gets better, and, this is a big one, the way you run the company gets better.

I hope you're beginning to realize that this book is not simply offering another way to get referrals. This book is about an overarching business strategy that can and—to operate at the highest levels—must infuse every department in your organization. A referral strategy is a lead strategy, it's a customer service strategy, it's a process strategy, it's a competitive strategy, it's a management strategy, it's a people strategy, and it's a financial strategy.

But most of all, it's a strategy designed to satisfy the logical and emotional needs of every prospect and customer.

CHAPTER 3

The Path to Referral

N ow that we've covered the realities of and the qualities of the referred business, it's time to start moving toward applying them to the strategic and tactical realities of your business.

The foundation we've built so far, along with the additional steps proposed in this chapter, will become your new point of view for improving the techniques you currently use and building entirely new ways to find, engage, and convert referrals.

Meet the 4 Cs of marketing

The world of marketing has changed dramatically in the last two decades, due in large part to how the Internet has changed the way we shop, network, and learn. These changes gave rise to the highly wired business, while making the personal nature of the highly engaged business even more impactful.

These changes require marketers, even successful ones, to adapt and evolve regularly. The age of the 4 Ps of marketing—calling for businesses to create products, test out pricing models, and place and promote them—has given way to the age of the customer. A new set of principles has shoved its way alongside product, price, place, and promotion in the hierarchy of marketing planning. In the age of the customer, the 4 Cs are the keys to business success: content, context, connection, and community.

Content

Authentic content that educates or is otherwise seen as valuable to the consumer is the new currency of marketing. Customers have grown weary of marketing messages that are blasted at them in an effort to sell. In fact, this type of marketing has little or no impact for most businesses, as prospects now have so many ways to completely shut it out. Any information that is seen by a prospect as irrelevant is increasingly blocked as they tread water in the daily flood of information.

Highly wired businesses, for example, often distribute detailed "how to" information for free, via blog posts and white papers, in an effort to gain the permission of the prospect to engage them in a sales conversation.

Boston-based HubSpot (www.hubspot.com), an online, inbound-lead-generation software service provider, takes this approach to incredible levels. HubSpot offer prospects dozens of white papers on Web design, search engine optimization, and traffic building. In addition, visitors to their Web site find useful tools such as the Web site grader that allows you to evaluate your site instantly, based on important search engine factors. On any given day you can drop by and catch a live or archived Web presentation on relevant small- and midsize-business Web marketing topics.

This no-strings-attached content allows them to break down built-in sales resistance, build trust, and demonstrate expertise in their business. Quite often this information is served up by search engines in response to very specific queries, adding another layer of trust to the content.

Content is not simply a buzzword created by new-media consultants; it's an important marketing strategy, and I see it consistently in widely referred businesses in the form of text, audio, video, and in-person presentations.

Context

While we now enjoy access to an enormous amount of information, we're also overwhelmed with the need to filter, aggregate, and make sense of it all.

The ability to situate information within the context of a prospect's life has become a core marketing tactic. In some cases, this can be accomplished by simplifying our messages and uncluttering our marketing communications. Creating products that do less but do it elegantly. Narrowing our ideal target customer focus. Condensing advice from reams of relevant data into snack-size digests.

The growth of blogs, and the ascension of some very high-profile bloggers, can be attributed in part to their presentation of high-quality information, frequently and in short bursts.

Two great examples of business owners who propelled themselves into high-growth business modes through the consistent sharing of content in blogs are Chris Brogan (www.chrisbrogan.com), founder of New Marketing Labs, and Brian Clark (www.copyblogger.com). Brogan and Clark both produce content worth reading on a daily basis and have turned the legions of readers that show up every day into lucrative writing, publishing, speaking, and consulting engagements.

The success of microblogging platforms such as Twitter, where millions of people go every day to answer "What I'm doing right now" in 140 characters or less, can also be attributed to our snack culture's desire for good information in as few words as possible.

Connection

Today, there is a touch of irony to the idea of connection as a business principle. The more connected we become through technology, the more we long for real connections involving live human interactions.

In his 1982 book *Megatrends*, John Naisbitt coined the phrase "high tech, high touch" to warn of a growing need to match every advance in technology with a corresponding human touch. Naisbitt's writing focused primarily on the interaction of machine versus man in the typical workplace, as it was written far in advance of the World Wide Web and many other forms of information technology.

However, the most remarkable businesses seem to innovate and create buzz by balancing high-tech connections with high-touch engagements, by allowing one to inform the other. By using technology to allow prospects to connect when and where they choose, they allow people to connect more deeply when and where they choose.

In 2002 management consultant and executive coach David Allen compiled his thoughts on productivity into a book he called *Getting Things Done*. Hundreds of books, software programs, planners, and training courses on the subject of time management and productivity have come in and out of fashion over the years, but Allen's book and the movementlike connection and community it spawned is nothing short of breathtaking.

His teachings and theories have gathered what some might call a cult following, spawning scores of Web sites, services, and popular blogs, such as 43folders (www.43folders.com), devoted to his simple yet powerful approach to planning and, well, getting things done.

Allen himself marvels at the connection his GTD approach has created with devotees; he claims all he did was figure out how to manage time with basic tools like a pen and paper, folders, and an inbox.

I asked him what he thought people connected with in his ideas that caused them to become involved at such a high level. "Some people need to focus on the bigger picture and get that clear, and a lot of people have a fire in their belly but they need to get down more on the runway and handle the projects and actions about them to make all of the stuff happen. I'm equally respective and irreverent of all of those.

"If you want to find God, great. If you need cat food, fabulous. It's all stuff to do."

Allen found a way to handle a modern problem, stress, with a simple, people-oriented system.

Community

The last of the 4 Cs is community. We've always had community—we find it in our neighborhoods, our schools, our churches, and our business organizations. But those forms of community are based on geography.

In the wired world, community is free to form around shared ideas, common interests, and strategic relationships unbound by distance.

Due to the ease of access to online tools, anyone, including our prospects, customers, partners, suppliers, mentors, and even competitors, can form communities to publish information, generate and distribute audio, video, or written content about our products and services, and play an active role in the overall impression a market has about our brand.

Community creation tools such as Squidoo (www.squidoo.com) and Ning (www.ning.com) empower fans of movies, bands, and brands to gather in club-type settings online to support their love of things like the Twilight Saga, rapper TechNine, and Mountain Dew. While a Chamber of Commerce afterhours networking event is indeed a place to build community, so too is the conversation in the comments on a blog post, on Twitter, in a Squidoo lens, or in a Ning-hosted community.

While the notion of community-building online has become a very commonplace practice, the opportunity for community-building offline is richer than ever. The local remodeling contractor that buys Christmas trees and holds a holiday party where customers come and choose a tree is providing an essential community-building opportunity. The consultant who routinely invites small groups of customers to lunch so they can network and share ideas with peers is providing an essential community-building opportunity. And finally, the independent book retailer that allows Scout groups and PTA committees to use its space for gathering and holding meetings is providing an essential community-building opportunity.

Widely referred businesses of all types create opportunities for customers and prospects to join a community.

What kind of business are you?

First, let's get a baseline assessment of where you are today. (If you are currently in the planning stages of your business, follow along, as this may change the way you think about your marketing planning.)

In my experience, successful businesses fall into one of two camps. Those businesses that rely on the evolution of marketing driven by social networking, content-rich Web sites and blogs, domination of local search-engine traffic, e-mail marketing, sophisticated use of customer relationship management software, and automated lead-nurturing and follow-up campaigns—in short, all that technology has to offer—are what I call wired, or tech-oriented, businesses. These businesses spend most of their marketing time online.

They have embraced the full set of high-tech tools spawned by ubiquitous access to the Internet and our growing reliance on Web searches for all manner of information. Global access to communities, speedy follow-up, and automated customer communications tools are hallmarks of the wired business. They network, but typically online, in communities based more on shared ideas than shared geography.

In the other camp are businesses that rely on more traditional, offline business-building tools, such as face-to-face selling, in-person relationships, local community involvement, Chamber of Commerce networking, and authentic storytelling, or engaged businesses. They rely on the human need for face-to-face, people-oriented relationships, in which handshakes and hugs still matter. They hire for people skills and the ability to impress a group during a presentation. They attend conferences, host workshops, and sponsor customer appreciation lunches.

Both of these models are effective ways to build a business and, depending on the industry you find yourself in, may be exactly the approach you've taken or plan to take in order to grow your business. In fact, I've rarely encountered a healthy business that doesn't enlist the business-building power of one of these approaches.

However, there is an increasing danger in relying solely on one or the other. If you are a mostly off-line business, content to sit on the Internet sidelines and ignore some of the more trendy-sounding online platforms, you will be overlooked by the growing percentage of your market that relies on the Internet exclusively to find the products and services they wish to buy. In addition, you will find it increasingly difficult to compete in a world where competitors can find and tap talent and resources from around the world.

On the other hand, businesses lacking an integrated approach that includes face-to-face selling and close customer contact, or that believe social media is the only worthwhile marketing strategy, may find it difficult to engage prospects and convert customers.

One tendency that is clear to me is that businesses that create the most buzz seem to have a knack for tapping and creating a convergence of these two models, the wonderful places where online and off-line strategies and tactics intersect and overlap, as an essential ingredient in their culture of referral.

Deborah Richmond, owner of the Michigan-based Internet marketing firm Tekkbuzz (www.tekkbuzz.com), left the following comment on a blog post I wrote asking readers to tell me what they do to get the biggest return on social media. I think it captures this idea of blending off-line with online for amplified results nicely.

> I get the biggest return for my business using social media when I combine my online activity with my off-line activity. One of my favorite strategies is to take the business cards I am given at face-to-face events and connect to these people on LinkedIn, Facebook, and Twitter. People I have met only once soon become good friends online, as I learn more about their businesses, careers, family, and hobbies.
>
> The next time I see them, we behave like old friends, asking about all the fun things we've learned about each other online. This combination of off-line and online networking is a terrific way to further relationships. Many of these people then come to me for consulting advice or refer other people my way.

Let me explain how each of these models unfolds in the real world, and then the steps involved in merging these tactics will make more sense.

The mostly online high-tech approach is, of course, often taken by businesses that are technology related, but it is the customer who usually dictates the model that companies adopt. Companies that depend upon marketing to large numbers of prospects, perhaps prospects located around the world, feel the need to rely heavily on technology, the Internet, and automation tools to reach out to prospects.

They choose pay-per-click or banner advertising as the primary method for creating awareness and generating leads. They may obsess over search-engine optimization, author a blog, and send monthly newsletters via e-mail. They may employ e-mail management systems, online forums, or intranets for internal communication. Their customer help desks are managed by employees located in various locations, including their own homes.

Some industries, such as insurance, for example, lend themselves more naturally to the characteristics of the off-line, high-touch business. These businesses succeed by building personal networks and deep customer relationships through the use of in-person selling skills.

While they make use of the Internet and technology in marketing, they are more likely to engage prospects at a Chamber of Commerce meeting or by presenting information in a seminar setting. They hold customer appreciation events, often meet in their customers' offices or homes, and employ a local staff that commutes to the office. This more traditional approach relies heavily on what business coach Dixie Gillaspie calls "hugs and handshakes" to develop customer relationships.

The converged business

I've spent time painting a picture of two successful yet distinct business models, one that relies heavily on the Internet and high-tech approaches and another steeped in traditional, people-based selling.

In my experience the online-based business almost always excels at the first two of the Cs of marketing—content and context—using technology. The off-line-focused business naturally gravitates to the more people-oriented connection and community.

A business model that focuses on making all four Cs an integral part of the customer experience, blending high-tech with high-touch tactics, is today's greatest opportunity for creating a business that turns into a referral engine.

The converged business uses every advance in technology as an opportunity to forge a deeper, more personal relationship with its customers. The important distinction here, much like Naisbitt suggested in *Megatrends*, is that the use of technology is combined with a bit of a human ballast and not used as a way to wall off communication or add convenience for the overworked customer service representative.

Instead, technology is used as a way to create larger networks, interact in ways that are most convenient for the customer, and engage customers more frequently.

For the converged, high-tech, high-touch business, the primary decision filter for every marketing process, customer touch point, and tactic is how technology can make the customer experience more fun, more convenient, more engaging, and more frequent.

Here's a simple example: A tech-oriented marketer may naturally use online Web conferences as opportunities to educate prospects, while a people-oriented marketer may naturally develop cobranded marketing materials with strategic partners as a way to actively refer business to each other.

The converged marketer combines these approaches by developing a series of topics and asking strategic partners to present each online educational workshop. The partners provide the content, participate in promoting the event, and promote the recorded version of the presentation. In addition, they create a blog and ask each of the partners to create content related to their specialty. The blog posts and archived recordings become a magnet for local search-engine traffic while promoting each of the participating businesses.

While doing research on this idea I had the opportunity to visit with Oregon-based personal image consultant Joanna Van Vleck, and I think she has created a pretty fine example of just such an innovation.

Van Vleck consults with men on their wardrobes, hair, and overall style. She found that while her clients loved working with her, they hated being dragged into stores to try on clothes—keep in mind these are all men. On one occasion a client suggested using a Web cam instead. He would buy the stuff on his own and consult with her about what worked with and what didn't via video conference. At first Van Vleck found the idea a bit odd, but somewhere along the way she discovered a brilliant innovation.

Today the Trunk Club (www.trunkclub.com), a unique consulting business she founded to take advantage of the use of video technology, helps men around the globe avoid doing something they hate—go shopping. (By the way, that's the surest way to create any meaningful point of differentiation.) The Trunk Club concept is pretty simple: When you need something to wear you get in touch with your Trunk Club expert; they pick out clothes based on style, need, and budget; and send them to your home or office. You try them on and get advice via video conference and pay for and keep only what you want. By the way, during our interview she shared that her little idea was poised to do around $3 million in its first year.

This is a business strategy with overarching implications for everything from hiring to product development, but you can apply its power simply by looking at individual marketing tactics and asking yourself how to add convergence—how you can make your engagement tactics more wired and your wired tactics more engaging.

Work-clothing maker Carhartt used this blended approach when it created its Tough Jobs blog (toughjobs.carhartt.com). Customers are invited to write in and describe how they put the company's clothing to the test on the job. They made the process fairly easy by creating an online submission form. Customers get to post their stories and the company gets to build and engage its customer community while creating content that its customers can relate to.

I was told by a consultant on this project that the idea came about when someone discovered boxes of notes, photos, and letters, written by hand, praising the company's products. Another great example of taking the human touch and using an available new technology to bring it to life.

The net effect of systematically applying this new thinking is a business that more easily builds trust, generates inbound leads, creates a culture of buzz, shortens the sales cycles, charges premium pricing, and grows to expect referrals from every single customer relationship.

Software company 37Signals (www.37signals.com) makes Web-based applications designed to ease collaboration, sharing, discussion, and getting work done. As one might assume, they are a high-tech venture living primarily on the Web. In fact, most of its fourteen-member staff works remotely. As users of the company's flagship product, Basecamp, generally attest, 37Signals is a different kind of software company.

Every product, every communication, and every feature is built to be simple, intuitive, and user-friendly. A snippet from the company's Web site illustrates this point of view quite well: "Software that requires training is failed software. Our products are intuitive. You'll pick them up in seconds or minutes, not hours, days or weeks. We don't sell you training because you don't need it."

Or, consider this quote from a presentation given by cofounder Jason Fried: "You don't need to outdo the competition. It's expensive and defensive. Underdo your competition. We need more simplicity and clarity."

While 37Signals is indeed a high-tech company, they've created a high-touch brand of customer loyalty by doing away with buzzwords, contracts, and hype in their marketing. While other Web app companies take years to become profitable, if they ever do, 37Signals has been able to make money from the very outset in a highly competitive marketplace.

And then of course there are opportunities to blend the online and off-line strategies and tactics in the business model itself.

Take for instance Seattle-based social networking community Biznik (www.Biznik.com). Biznik is a community of entrepreneurs and business owners, but it's not another LinkedIn. Biznik members connect and network online, but then they meet in person. Biznik features the standard suite of online tools. Members can build a profile, submit articles, and republish their blog and Twitter streams to their profile page. However, the entire site is organized to allow members to join and participate in geography-based groups and communities. In addition, members can host and promote in-person live events using the community-based promotion tools.

According to Biznik cofounder Lara Eve Feltin, the platform is a hybrid of an online social network and member-driven local face-to-face events. While networking in social platforms is very efficient, moving what's often a surface relationship into a strategic partner or customer takes a lot of effort. A service like Biznik makes that crucial trust-building next step of meeting face-to-face much easier.

High-tech way to connect, learn, and enroll; high-touch way to build trust, engage, and do business.

The ideal customer life cycle

Look at your current practices. How can this converged model come to life in your business? If you're just getting started, you may find it quite easy to adopt this new way of thinking. Businesses that are deeply rooted in highly wired or highly engaged practices, however, often find it difficult to change how they look at their customer relationships and marketing tactics.

I've developed something I call the Ideal Customer Lifecycle as a tool to demonstrate the way a prospect becomes a customer, and that customer becomes a referral source, in an effort to break the transition into a converged business into some practical steps.

There are seven stages of referral development and corresponding touch points along the customer life cycle.

Know

This is the initial introduction to your company, and while it is commonly conveyed through your advertising messages, it is also the point at which a referred lead discovers you. The cliché "You only get one chance to make a good impression" applies here. The best way to start the relationship is to communicate a clear brand or point of differentiation that is designed to attract your ideal customer and your ideal referral sources.

It's essential that you have narrowly defined what an ideal customer looks like for your business, so that you can speak as directly as possible to that customer in all of your communications.

Look very closely at the messages contained in your advertising, media kits, and marketing materials.

Like

Once a lead is aware of your company, they can and should be led to dig a little deeper, to see what's behind the ads. This is often the point when your Web presence or physical presence (store, offices, marketing materials, etc.) set the tone for a deeper connection. Without a defined process for getting to know more about your company without any commitment, without the opportunity to lurk and learn a little before pulling out a credit card, prospects tend to hold back from becoming customers.

Take a walk around your office: Does it send the right message? What about your logo, store design, uniforms, trucks: Do they invite prospects to move forward? What message does your Web site send? What happens when a prospect in this phase Googles you? Are you sending educational messages and contacts via tools such as an online newsletter?

Trust

When a prospect is ready to learn more (this may be by agreeing to a face-to-face meeting or signing up to receive your biweekly newsletter), you are approaching the trust hurdle. This is for some the trickiest spot. When a lead is referred to your business, you borrow some trust from the referral source, but you can easily lose that trust if your initial attempts to engage the prospect don't connect. You can't simply assume that because Uncle Bob referred a friend, that friend is ready to buy from you.

Your marketing materials and sales presentations must be designed to communicate your core message of differentiation with complete clarity. During the trust-building phase your prospect may need to be nurtured for a time. What kinds of educational opportunities, such as free reports, "how-to" checklists, and information-rich seminars can you offer?

Everyone in the company who comes into contact with a customer or a prospect is performing a trust-building or -eroding practice. Can everyone on the organization deliver your core message in a confident and consistent manner? Repetition builds trust; trust builds the brand.

Try

Far too often companies think of their offerings exclusively in terms of the core product or service: We are a law firm, so people retain us when they need a lawyer. This approach limits your exposure to vast pockets of prospects and usually leads to customers who are less than ideal.

One of the best ways to ensure that every customer relationship evolves into a referral relationship is to create a way for your customers to sample your business and in turn give your business the opportunity to sample the customer. The purest path to referral momentum is one that leads every prospect to determine, beyond the shadow of a doubt, whether your company has the answer or, and this is equally important, whether it does not—an educated yes or no is the answer we are after.

If the only path a prospect can take is directly from sales pitch to buy, then a third option creeps into the mix—indifference. Indifference is what leads to customers who come and go for price, make unreasonable demands, and push you outside of your core value proposition. Fail to serve a customer like this—and you will—and they will certainly tell ten friends not to hire you.

The use of trial offers, seminars, evaluations, guarantees, and any type of activity that provides a prospect with the ability to sample your products and services effectively before making what may be a costly purchase can make a customer much more comfortable and allow you to demonstrate how you work.

Providing lower-priced products and services to support and supplement your core service is a great way to reach markets that may not be ready to buy or simply don't have enough experience with your company to determine if they should go with you. This is often a significant problem when you compete with better-known organizations. By offering the low-risk trial you can gain the upper hand.

I once worked with an architect who created a $499 feasibility audit that builders and property owners could employ to get a quick opinion of the potential zoning issues, regulatory snags, and rough per-foot building costs before they invested in a full-fledged set of plans or proposals. The money that customers paid was barely enough to cover the architect's time, but it gave them a real advantage if a project was to move forward—so who do you think started making the short list for projects they performed the audit service on?

Buy

Finally, we get to sell the primary products and services. Yes, it's essential that you have a product or service that people like, deliver as promised, and gets people talking. But from a referral standpoint, it's the process of becoming a customer that needs the work. How you orient your customer once they say yes is a referral marketing touch point. How you fulfill the order, how you deliver the order, how you communicate throughout the process, how you communicate after the project, and how you ask to be paid for the work are all elements that determine whether you are referral-worthy or not in the eyes of your customer.

In this stage, expectations are everything. No matter what you think is good or bad, if it's not what the customer expected, it can raise a red flag. For example, you might be rather haphazard about getting your bills out and think, "Well, the customer won't mind if I don't bill them as promptly as promised," but to the customer this can signal sloppiness on your part (not to mention disaster from a cash-flow standpoint).

Do you have an orientation process? A kit of information that explains everything and identifies everyone the new customer needs to know in case of problems or in order to move forward? Is there a clean process by which a project is handed from the sales team to the service team? (Even if that's the same person, it's a process that's important.)

Repeat

If you do a good job with the previous stage, you are halfway toward tapping the repeat phase for all the power it's worth. The key factor in creating repeat sales, expanded product sales, and long-term loyalty is to make certain that your customers are getting the most value possible from your products and services.

When someone buys your product or service, commit to teaching them the proper way to get the most from it. You can teach them over time how to do this. You can teach them how to move up to the next level of your product or service. You can teach them the secret hacks, the under-the-hood tips, and you can even expose them to the best practices of your other customers.

Far too often we sell a product or service and just assume our customers are getting the results they desired or were promised. By creating a systematic set of "how-to" materials, we can help them be more successful, use more of the features, and ultimately experience greater value.

And that's what generates referrals.

Finally, it's essential that your customer-fulfillment process also contain a step that forces you to ascertain and review with your customer the value they received from your product or project. This is a great way to fix gaps in service with specific customers and gain invaluable research on how to get better at every stage.

Do you have a results review process? Do you have routine continuing education to point out advanced features or cross-sell other products and services?

Refer

The last stage of the customer referral life cycle is for your customers to become such total advocates for your business that they operate as a form of uncompensated sales staff. You know you have built a Referral Engine when this type of action becomes common within your customer base. The ultimate goal is to lead every customer to this place.

Even if referrals are flowing freely into your lead system now, there are ways to stimulate and facilitate even greater amounts of referrals. At this stage you should focus on making it very easy for your advocates to participate in your business, come together as a community, and tap your entire network.

For example, you can create peer-to-peer discussion panels that allow some of your greatest customer fans to discuss solutions and challenges with prospects. Or you can create customer advisory and referral boards that allow them to participate in the formation of your marketing campaigns and business strategies. Hold events that focus on networking and referral opportunities. Develop educational seminars and systematically introduce your strategic partner network to your customers.

The customer touch point map

You may find it helpful to create a touch point map to identify every potential customer (touch point) and a corresponding marketing tactic related to that contact. In many cases you will be identifying tactics and touch points that may not exist yet, so this map can become an important guide for future marketing development. (For an example of a customer touch point map, go to www.referralenginebook.com.)

As you create your map and each contact point, keep the important concepts of content, context, connection, and community—and ultimately convergence—firmly in mind.

For many, this is the first step to becoming more referable. In the next chapter we will outline the steps involved in building a marketing system centrally focused on referral generation. In subsequent chapters we will dive deeply into each step on the way to helping you design the marketing system that turns your business into a widely referred business.

An expanded view of collaboration

As I've stated throughout this book, the Web has changed many things about business, but one thing's for sure: It has dramatically enhanced our ability to collaborate with every important constituency group.

When most small-business owners think collaboration, they generally limit this thinking to the kind of collaboration you might naturally do with a supplier while completing some aspect of a project, or perhaps a strategic partner required to mesh together a complex solution. But in today's social media world, the concept of collaboration has expanded to encompass a much more overall strategic role.

In fact, collaboration with prospects, customers, partners, providers, staff, mentors, and perhaps even competitors can play a key role. Technology enables any business, regardless of size, to orchestrate great collaborative efforts, dramatically increasing your effectiveness and efficiency. This expanded view of collaboration represents an entirely new way to think about engaging your markets, building connection and community, and empowering your staff to deliver on your marketing promise.

Finding ways to employ collaboration systematically at every level of your business isn't that difficult once you shift your mind to this way of thinking. The following examples demonstrate ways to use collaboration tools to generate buzz among every important constituency.

With prospects

The expectation of the opportunity to collaborate has become so commonplace that companies need to consider it with prospective customers.

Collaboration tools that allow prospects to rate and review content on your site, for example by posting videos or making comments on blog posts, can create an initial engagement and add to the overall conversation. Inviting and using feedback from someone who is in the information-gathering stage, or perhaps has decided not to buy from you, is a great way to understand how to get better at marketing. Free or low-cost scripts such as those from JSKit (www.js-kit.com) allows Web site owners to install voting, rating, and review buttons alongside content on their sites.

Monitoring Twitter for brand mentions, comments, and complaints has become a standard marketing practice by organizations large and small. Many companies provide a significant amount of customer support through this platform. Customers ask questions and direct replies to a company support account.

As a referral practice, this is a great way to demonstrate publicly how you respond to customer and prospect inquiries.

By creating and adding content to a blog you can take advantage of the software's built-in features to engage prospects in a conversation and effectively collaborate on the creation of content. Many blog owners find that by asking for opinions, tips, or suggestions from readers related to the topic of the post, they can create much richer content while building a more active readership.

With customers

Every business should invest in a low-cost video camera to start capturing customer success stories and testimonials. The Flip camera costs less than two hundred dollars and slips into a pocket or purse so easily that every person who calls on customers should have one.

Once you shoot the video, you can use video Web-hosting sites such as YouTube (www.youtube.com) or Viddler (www.viddler.com) to upload, host, and stream your video on your Web site, just by pasting a few simple lines of html code.

Another effective customer collaboration strategy involves a kind of peer-to-peer selling. Using Web-conferencing services such a Go-ToMeeting (www.gotomeeting.com) you can invite a select group of customers to share or even demonstrate their experiences with your products and solutions with a group of prospects.

This is not a selling session but a chance for peers to discuss challenges, trends, and approaches.

Customers who enjoy the interaction created through the peer-to-peer approach may also enjoy giving you feedback on marketing materials, strategic plans, new product ideas, and how user-friendly (or not) your Web site is.

Online survey tools, such as those from Survey Monkey (www .surveymonkey.com) or Survey Gizmo (www.surveygizmo.com) are another great way to easily collect information and opinions and collaborate with your current customers.

With partners

Your strategic partners, particularly those who do or can refer business to you, offer some nice opportunities for collaborations that can generate more referrals and add to the quality and quantity of content you can produce. If you have built relationships with businesses that complement your offerings, you can partner with them to create workshops and seminars that appeal to an audience beyond your own network of prospects and customers.

Recording interviews with industry leaders is a great way to create valuable content and gain access to new partners who have become intrigued by your offer to interview them. Many businesses have found that creating a podcast, an audio show that is housed online and can be syndicated to platforms such as iTunes, is a great way to raise their exposure and credibility.

Much like the Carhartt customer blog mentioned previously, another powerful collaboration tactic is the creation of a blog network. In this case a heating and cooling contractor in Boise, Idaho, might create a blog called Boise Home Repair and invite strategic partners, such as an electrician, a plumber, a lawn service, and a painter to contribute content related to their specific areas of expertise. Partners may view it as a way to gain added exposure, the blog's content will flourish as the group contributes, and the person looking for home repair providers in Boise, Idaho, is going to have little trouble finding this site when they go online to search.

With providers

Project collaboration in a world of global business has become a must. Thankfully, due to suites of tools such as Central Desktop (www .centraldesktop.com), Microsoft's Office Live Workspace (workspace .officelive.com), and Google Docs (docs.google.com), that allow groups of people to work on documents, assign tasks, and track milestones remotely, it's also become pretty easy to do.

Online project collaboration with service providers makes collaboration much more efficient and creates opportunities to access providers from anywhere in the world.

With staff

Another group that doesn't always get mentioned in discussions on collaboration is an organization's staff. As more and more people work remotely, it becomes much more important to use tools that allow your staff to work as effectively as if they were side by side. Obviously this also allows you to recruit talent from any part of the world.

"Mind-mapping" tools that facilitate and organize random ideas, such as MindMeister (www.mindmeister.com), allow groups of people to brainstorm and collaborate without needing to gather together.

An operations manual is a necessary but often overlooked tool. Online collaboration tools such as Central Desktop make it very easy for numerous members of a staff to create, edit, and update a company operations manual or set of processes, all from within a Web browser. Documenting your organization's success systems, much of which may reside exclusively in the brain of a handful of employees, is a critical collaboration step.

Using e-mail management tools, like E-mail Center Pro (www

.e-mailcenterpro.com), allows organizations to handle e-mail follow-up collaboratively. With an e-mail management tool in place, several individuals can monitor all of the mail that comes to, say, support@ yourcompany.com and track which ones have received a response. You can even write common response templates for consistent replies.

Simply communicating with a staff that may not be in the same location can present some challenges. Employing a service like Jott (www.jott.com) that allows you to create lists of employees and then send the entire list an e-mail simply by speaking your message into the phone can make instant and spontaneous communication with staff much easier. I've also used this tool to send a meeting overview to a client as I drive back to my office.

Your marketing organized

One of the most difficult tasks for small-business owners when it comes to marketing is organization. In this case I'm not talking about the clutter on your desk as much as the clutter in your thinking. Until you start to look at marketing as one of the core systems in your business, it will always feel like a disjointed and disconnected thing that you know you should do when you get around to it. And that's no way to build referral momentum.

I find that it's helpful for many people to look at marketing in the traditional org chart fashion. Even if it's just you and the intern. Here's why: No matter how many actual people you have in your organization, your business has many necessary functions. The problem is that without a map that helps you understand the important role of each of these functions many simply don't get the focus they deserve.

By creating an organization chart that explicitly acknowledges all the functions that need to be performed, you stand a far greater chance of developing individual systems and strategies to make sure the work in each area is organized and done. Not to mention the fact that you can lay the foundation for growth and a consistent experience if and when you have the bodies to add more boxes to your chart.

To keep your org chart simple, for now start with Marketing, Money, and Management at the top. To see how to expand from there, see the example of a marketing organization chart at www.referralenginebook .com.

If you can see that your company's marketing system does indeed need to perform all of the functions listed above, you may more easily grasp how to craft processes to move each and every customer along the path to becoming a hypersatisfied source of referrals.

And that's the way to build marketing momentum!

CHAPTER 4

The Referral System View

So far we have covered how to establish a strong foundation for a widely referred business. We've laid the groundwork. It is my hope that the discussion to this point has already help create a significant shift in the way you view your business as a whole. Now it's time to actually build your systematic referral-generation program.

In Chapter 3, I introduced the realities of this brave new world of marketing we find ourselves in and presented a map of the path followed by a prospect on the way to becoming a referral source. Visualizing the linear and logical path of a client's experience can open your eyes to the potential ways a prospect can get off track.

In this chapter we will see an overview of the referral system process, and we will get very specific with each step in subsequent chapters.

Your authentic strategy

There are over a dozen steps in the creation of an authentic referral strategy, but first we should introduce the concepts of the *core talkable difference* and the *narrowly defined ideal customer*.

These two ingredients must be carefully blended to create your overall referral strategy. On the surface, you might think that I'm simply referring to the tried-and-true practices of defining a target market and developing a core message. Instead, you'll find that a highly converged, widely referred business dives into these two key activities in a much more active way.

You'll start by defining your ideal customer and core message, but you'll also rethink every process in your business from the perspective of your chosen strategy. Eventually, you will shape a culture of referral, crafting a profoundly remarkable customer, partner, and employee experience.

Core talkable difference

The first step in the design of your referral system is to unearth the simple, remarkable difference that is your chief competitive advantage. It's not enough to offer a nice feature, something your competition doesn't; this must be something so special that people can't help talking about your business. End of discussion. If the core difference you offer doesn't make people stop and take notice, you've still got work to do. I can't stress enough how significant this first step is to the eventual success (or failure) of your referral ambitions.

Genuine talkable differences lay dormant in many businesses, hiding in the places they least expect. It's rarely about a game-changing innovation; often it's a new way to look at your business, a new way to talk about results, or a new way to give exceptional service to a narrow target audience.

Though it may not be the next iPod, the difference must be extraordinary. As I've heard my friend Scott Ginsberg, the name-tag guy, say, "There are no cover bands in the Rock and Roll Hall of Fame." Talkable differences must be original, real, and compelling. It's not enough to be an accountant who gets the tax return done before April 15 or your money back. If you want people to talk, you've got to be the accountant who gets the tax return done before April 15, then gets your oil changed at the car wash next door while you discuss your return in his office.

Many times business owners and marketers look for ways to create innovations and points of differentiation through elaborate technical add-ons or by attempting to create entirely new product or service categories. From my experience, one of the best ways to create an innovation or differentiation for your business is to take something people already realize they may want and need and make it even easier to want, need, and understand. In fact, the true test of this theory is when you can create something so simply brilliant that people can and do explain it to their friends with ease.

I witnessed a stunning example of this on a trip to California.

Pizza is a pretty mature category. Delivery was a huge innovation in the industry years ago, but it seems like tinkering with the crust and baking variations is all that's left to work on.

The Cheeseboard Pizza Collective (www.cheeseboardcollective .coop), in Berkeley, California, has created a dead-simple innovation and incredible point of differentiation, and it's made for a very healthy, buzz-worthy business.

The core talkable difference is this. Instead of serving up a menu of pizza variations and cooking each to order, the restaurant offers one unique pizza each day as the only menu item. I was there on a Friday night and the line for pizza ran out the door and down the street for some distance. Patrons order any amount of the pizza they like at twenty dollars per pizza and, as seating is very limited, often plop down outside the store to eat picnic-style while listening to a live jazz trio. The fixed menu, fixed price, and make-it-in-quantity approach allows the collective to serve thousands a day, and the pizza was one of the best I've ever eaten. While it would be difficult to capture the cultlike following this place seems to enjoy, it sure looks like a concept waiting to be duplicated elsewhere!

A couple of other important mentions that add to the differentiation: The pizzas are always vegetarian (narrowing their market a bit, but hey, it's Berkeley). They use high-end ingredients, such as organic cremini mushrooms and goat cheese, as their business model allows them to make great margins. The business model, as the name suggests, is a collective. All twelve employees own the business, are paid the same, manage the business, ring the registers, bake the pies, and wash the dishes. Profits are shared and reinvested in the business.

The insurance giant Aflac (www.aflac.com) is a nice example of a company that built a talkable (quackable) reputation, though also an odd but very memorable marketing campaign. The company introduced the now famous Aflac duck campaign in 2000 and turned the quacking duck into an Advertising Hall of Fame icon that's both endearing to customers and the bottom line.

Mark Combs, a Florida-based account manager for Aflac, shared this about his company, "I love that I work for a company that is so widely recognized and enjoys such a solid reputation. I wear my name tag almost everywhere. It's fun to hear folks walk behind me and quack, and I love being asked, 'Where's your duck?' or 'What's the duck doing?' Could you ask for a better conversation starter?"

So how could you strip what your business or industry does, something people already get, down to a simple innovation, and create an innovation that anyone can understand, buy, remember, and talk about?

Unfortunately, some businesses, even those experiencing a measure of success, may never capture the full impact of a remarkable difference unless they are willing to change how they do what they do, or at least reposition what it is that they do.

Either way, my experience is that while this step is vital, it's also very difficult for many businesses. While being different gets you talked about, it can feel very uncomfortable, or even risky. Would you be willing to wear a name tag every day of your life?

How to create a surefire innovation

If you find yourself scratching your head thinking, "We don't have a talkable innovation; how do I create one?" Consider the following criteria as you brainstorm potential ideas either as a new direction for your firm or as you craft your start-up.

The owner is the customer. Understanding the characteristics, desires, and behaviors of a narrowly defined target market is very hard work but essential to your success. Every marketing book or expert will tell you this, but few can give you the magic tablet that allows you to go deeply into the psyche of your prospect.

You can acquire some measure of knowledge from various research techniques but nothing beats living, breathing, and feeling the same things your prospects do. Some of the surest successes in history have come from founders who created a product or service to meet a personal need and discovered a business by virtue of doing so.

The market already understands the offering. Some entrepreneurs dream of locking themselves in a padded room for a year or so and emerging with the world's greatest innovation. Sounds romantic, I know, but if your innovation simply solves an incredible problem people don't yet know they have, you may wind up burning through the money before they get it.

Better to innovate around a proven market, borrow genius from an unrelated industry, or discover an unmet need in a mature market crying for a solution.

The market already spends money here. Sometimes marketers shy away from competition. If market research shows that there's too much competition in a given area or industry, the thinking is that the market is saturated and there's probably no room for your start-up there.

To that I say, nonsense. While it may be true that your neighborhood couldn't possibly stand another coffee shop, I've found the success of several businesses in an industry, even in the same direct community, can spell opportunity.

If people are already spending money on a product or service then two thirds of your work is done. They understand and value the offering enough to whip out their wallets. All that's left for you to do now is show them how much better you can make the experience. Few businesses really provide great service. In fact, stealing market share in mature markets is one of the easiest paths for smart start-ups to run.

It's an innovation that simplifies something. Much of this advice has focused on entering proven markets. While that's absolutely the advice I'm giving here, know that you must do so with a significant point of differentiation that the market easily understands and appreciates. In most cases this can be done by looking at the way most folks in the chosen market operate and find a way to simplify your offerings around breaking the mold.

For example, if people in your service business operate by proposal and bid, come up with a fixed price. If the traditional operating method is custom work, come up with a series of prepackaged offerings that meet most people's needs without the custom hassle.

The pizza restaurant described above that has one unique pizza on the menu each day. They make it up in big batches and serve thousands a day at twenty dollars per pie. Pretty simple approach, would you say?

Nothing is precious. Here's the one that can snag small business founders. If you're in love with your bright shiny baby start-up and all that it offers, you may become blind to the reality the market suggests. Keeping an open mind and a willingness to discover what the market really wants and adapt accordingly is one of the core advantages of your smallness—remember to use it.

Keep talking to your customers, your competitors, and your employees and remember that nothing is precious but what the numbers prove to be so.

The ideal referral customer

Not every prospect is an ideal fit for your business. Until you accept the notion that you must keep your market focus tight, you will constrict your organization's ability to grow. It's ironic, but by acknowledging whom you don't want to attract as a customer, you open greater opportunities for customer growth by way of referral.

This may appear to be an elitist point of view, but it's really the opposite. You can't possibly design a product or service to be all things to all people. By facing that reality up front and focusing on those to whom you truly can deliver a positive result, you're doing everyone a huge favor. "No, we don't do that here, but I have a great recommendation for you" might be the most powerful words you can say to a potential customer.

I've rarely worked with a business that did not have the ability to look at their customer base and acknowledge, "You know, if we had ten more customers just like this, life would be great." An ideal customer description is almost always lurking inside your existing customer base, and the quickest way to find them is to look at the customers that already refer business to you. Some combination of the solutions they were seeking, how they were introduced to your firm, their industry or size, and the way you have worked together is the ideal combination for your best work. Therefore, they had a great experience and now refer others to you.

This data is the starting place for changing how you think about what makes an ideal customer and, by virtue of that, understanding what doesn't.

The inbound referral process

In traditional business models, marketers generally go out and hunt for customers. They do it with advertising; they do it with sales pitches; they do it with trade shows and networking efforts.

In a fully functioning referral marketing system, the emphasis is moved from finding to being found, creating valuable content, engagement, and interaction where the ideal prospects are already looking. The dramatic rise in the use of search engines in our daily lives has made being found a vital element in the marketing of every type of business.

This is a very significant mind-set, one that is central to the highly converged business. Instead of whacking bushes for game, you begin lighting the candles lining the many paths that lead home. No one ever really liked being hunted or shouted at in the first place, and caller ID, TiVo, e-mail filtering, pop-up blockers, Do Not Call registries, CAN-SPAM, and satellite radio all owe their existence in some part to our desire to block out unwanted messages.

An inbound approach to creating awareness by providing valuable free content will amplify your referral strategy. Education-based marketing is often reserved for direct marketing and customer outreach through sales and lead-generation efforts, but we will expand this approach to include the education of your strategic partners and staff.

The customer network

A fully developed referral system targets two distinct prospect groups. The first is your customer base, or what I call your "direct network." The second, potentially richer, group is made up of other business that also serve your ideal customer who could be motivated to partner with you in some way to exchange referrals and support your customers. As you develop the tactical elements of your system you'll devise unique processes to engage each group.

Your customers are naturally qualified to act as your volunteer referral sales force. After all, they have experienced your brilliance firsthand! This line of thinking is absolutely correct, particularly with your newfound focus on attracting the ideal customer, but fully exploiting this group as a referral source requires a little more than simply asking your customers if they "know anybody who needs what you got."

The strategic partner network

I've spent some time developing this idea of an ideal target customer for your business. By drawing a complete picture of your ideal customer, you are more fully prepared to teach others how to spot and ultimately refer that ideal customer to your business. That's where the partner network comes into play. While many businesses focus the bulk of their referral-generation efforts on existing customers, the real untapped referral opportunity resides with strategic partners.

In a recent survey I conducted on referrals, respondents felt that less than 30 percent of their referrals came from strategic partners—I think that should be more like 60 percent.

Now, understand that I think it is absolutely vital that you first focus on thrilling customers so completely that every single one of them wants to go out of their way to refer others to your business. But once you've done that, you can engage strategic partners who may easily have the ability to introduce your business to hundreds or even thousands of qualified prospects at any given time. That, to me, is what makes developing a strategy and a set of tactics focused on strategic partners so essential.

The idea of partnering with businesses that have your same target market as customers is not a new one, but it's just gotten so much easier to do. By using technologies such as online Web conferencing and podcasting you can easily tap the knowledge and resources of a large group of experts and partners and make the knowledge available to your customers on demand.

Fulfilling the promise

It's one thing to create a brilliant plan of attack; it's another thing altogether to actually execute it. There are millions of great ideas written on napkins stuck in the desk drawers of would-be entrepreneurial superstars. The only worthwhile idea is the one on which you take action.

In this phase of the system you'll design the processes needed to consistently ask for referrals, involve your customers and partners in referral generation, and develop the creative offers that help motivate your referral sources to action.

Even though your referral sources may be willing and able to refer you, you still need to help motivate and stimulate them. Money for referrals is a crummy motivation, but a creative, on-message offer that turns referrals into a game is a great way to motivate them. Of course, saying thank you never hurts either.

After working out your motivation strategy, you'll create a referral follow-up process to ensure that referred leads are treated with special care, and that your referral sources are shown real appreciation to keep them motivated. While these processes may not seem like integral parts of your core product or service offerings, they are essential if you want to build real referral momentum.

Referral entry points

I assume you've also realized, of course, that it's not enough to simply design the parts of a system. You've also got to design the processes and routines necessary to operate the system as well. The following entry points are important to keep in mind as you also think in terms of how you operate your referral system in the real world.

Get an expectation mind-set. The first step is to believe that you deserve referrals. In fact, you are doing your customers and network a disservice by not giving them an easy path to bring the tremendous value of your products and services to those who need it. If you can't get past this psychological obstacle, any system you devise will break down under the weight of your self-consciousness.

The expectation mind-set must pervade your entire organization— it's everyone's job to find leads and convert them into customers. In addition, your lead-conversion process must contain referral generation as part of the deal: "We know you are going to be so satisfied with what we've agreed upon today that after the project is completed, we are going to schedule a meeting to make certain you received the results promised, and at that time we'll ask you if you would introduce us to three others that you know need these same results."

Now some might find the above statement hard to say, but I'm telling you it's the most positive marketing message you can utter: We know you are going to be so happy you will happily refer us. You've still got to deliver, but when you do you've established referrals as an expectation and condition in the relationship. It really is that simple.

Segment customers from partners. You need completely different referral approaches and offers for customers and strategic partners. By targeting your approach to these segments you can more easily develop programs that make sense and motivate for the right reasons.

For customers, the likely motivation is that they like what you do so much they want to refer you. You simply need to stay top of mind and make it easy for them to do. Hint: Ask and remind!

For partners, the motivation is quite different. Your job here is to effectively position referring you in a way that helps them add value to the relationships they already have with their customer. The simplest way to do that is to create valuable content, perhaps in the form of a white paper or seminar, and offer it to them to share it, cobranded, with their customers. You've just made it easy for them to do something they know they should be doing.

Create turnkey tools. Put tangible referral tools in the hands of your referral sources. Create documents that teach them the characteristics of your ideal customer, the trigger phrases your customers use when they need you, and your referral process.

Any business can create coupons and gift certificates and give them to their referral sources. A wine shop and caterer can create jointly branded marketing materials to help promote package deals. A bridal photographer can bring together a flower shop, a cake shop, a dress shop, and a DJ to write blog posts about cool weddings. Again, make it easy and it will happen.

Plan for logical collection. The place that referral systems fail most often is in the collection phase. Expectations are set, customers are thrilled, the referral motivation is in place, but nobody thinks to actually *ask* for the referral—d'oh! The best time to collect referrals from customers is at the point when they realize and acknowledge a good job was done. Create processes, such as annual results reviews, project reviews, and satisfaction surveys, and introduce or remind your customers about your referral programs during these reviews. This is also a great way to really find out what kind of job you're doing and correct course accordingly.

More than one creative entry point. Not all motivations are created equal. You must have multiple referral opportunities to take advantage of the hyperloyal customer who wants to set up a lunch to introduce your firm, the casual customer who needs the gift certificate mailing as a reminder, and the nonprofit agency partner that would love to run a promotion with you to benefit their cause and promote you to their members. Start with one or two referral program offers and gradually build new ones to let everyone find a way to play.

Measure and adjust. Create a dashboard of key referral indicators as a way to set goals and measure the success of your referral initiatives. So what are the key metrics? Page views, referred leads, appointments, closed deals? Watch those indicators that will help you see where your programs might be breaking down. You may be receiving referrals but not closing them, or you might be closing every referred lead, but there aren't enough of them.

This is a place you might consider going back to your referral sources to discuss your referral campaigns, the type of ideal customer you are focused on, the best way to make an introduction to your firm, and your total product or service offerings. What you learn from your measurement practices may help you adjust and create better educational tools.

Over the span of the next few chapters you will get the opportunity to dive deeply into each of the elements described in this referral system overview.

CHAPTER 5

Your Authentic Strategy

In this chapter I will share more than a dozen elements to mix and match for your referral strategy. You may not employ every element today, but over time you will tweak your ingredients to find the perfect combination for your business.

As you work your way through this chapter, make a note of the individual strategy parts that resonate with you most, even if you're not sure how you will integrate them. The goal of this chapter is to help you create a business strategy with the vibrancy to energize your staff, attract more of your ideal customers, deepen customer engagement, and solidify your own commitment to a business that feeds your sense of purpose.

One word of warning: This may be the most difficult, but also the most important, step in creating your referral marketing business system. In this stretch I am going to ask you to dig a little deeper personally than I have up to this point. I'm going to ask you to think about connecting what your business does, who it serves, what value it brings, and ultimately why someone would refer you, with what feels authentic to you. I know this kind of talk can get touchy-feely pretty fast, but you can't really expect much in the way of referral results if you don't believe in your referral strategy 100 percent. And you won't if it's not authentic.

In other words, you should feel comfortable driving the Referral Engine you build.

The higher purpose

There are three ingredients necessary for a rewarding and successful business experience: You must enjoy what you do and feel a sense of purpose; you must be good at what you do; and you must be able to convince other people to pay you for what you do.

I've met some very happy business people who seem to have the first two in abundance, but who can't quite figure out how to monetize them. But I've rarely come across a truly successful business owner who is happy making lots of money doing something they are good at without a deep-seated sense of purpose.

There is no way around it, really. Businesses that get talked about are driven by a higher purpose, one formed by a passionate owner or by a passionate team mission. Now, before I go much deeper here, I want to clarify that this notion of higher purpose does not necessarily suggest some spiritual or religious inspiration. It's more about creating something people want to connect with. It's an honesty that is hard to define but can't be faked. You usually know you've come across a business that's in touch with a higher purpose simply by the way you react to their story. It's not really what you do as much as why you do it that must be captured and defined as part of a truly captivating purpose.

In 2006 an American traveler, Blake Mycoskie, befriended children in Argentina and found they had no shoes to protect their feet. Wanting to help, he created TOMS Shoes (www.tomsshoes.com), a company that would match every pair of shoes purchased by giving a pair of new shoes to a child in need. One for one. Blake returned to Argentina with a group of family, friends, and staff later that year with ten thousand pairs of shoes made possible by TOMS customers.

In a *BusinessWeek* interview, Mycoskie shared what led him to create TOMS: "At first all I wanted to do with my new business was to be able to give kids in Argentina shoes. I didn't want to start a charity. I wanted to self-fund the venture. So I came up with the buy-one-give-one-away model. I based it on the idea that if I could sell a pair of shoes for forty dollars, I could make a good pair of shoes and give another pair away. I wanted to build it in a way that it could sustain itself.

"My thinking was that TOMS would show that entrepreneurs no longer had to choose between earning money or making a difference in the world. I wanted to prove that conscious capitalism is a viable business model for innovators worldwide, and entrepreneurs can focus on being ambassadors of humanity."

Sarah Endline didn't know she wanted to be in the candy business, but she did know that she wanted to start a business that was driven by socially responsible business practices. She had determined by the age of twenty-one that her life path would be that of a social entrepreneur, an entrepreneur who creates a product and a company steeped in socially responsible action. She earned her MBA at Harvard, where she studied the cases of companies like Ben & Jerry's and The Body Shop, but never quite found the model for her social venture. She took her business training and went to work at Yahoo!, her "change the world" fire still glowing. In 2004 she decided that the candy industry lacked an ethical and environmentally friendly player like the ice cream industry had in Ben & Jerry's. After traveling around the world to learn what she could about making chocolate in a socially responsible way, she launched sweetriot in the fall of 2005.

"I asked myself what I could work at twenty-four hours a day and still be happy and passionate about," Endline told me. "Chocolate just seemed to me the perfect answer." Sweetriot's stated mission is "to create a more just and celebrated multicultural world for our next generation." Sounds ambitious enough, but it's how it manifests in seemingly every aspect of the business that makes people take notice and get connected.

Their product is all-natural and healthy, and so is their business. "We create sweet experiences for our customers, partners, and employees," Endline told me. A documented sense of higher purpose for your business can often be stated by answering this question: What perception, perhaps even one word, do you want your customers to hold when they think of your business? You may or may not ever communicate the stated higher purpose for your business—it should quite naturally hang from most everything you do—but in terms of an actual statement or phrase it is also quite natural to hold it as an internal rallying cry.

Nobody does that

One of the surest strategies for creating a talked-about business is putting the emphasis on innovation. Innovation is a loaded word for some, because it conjures up notions of creating an entirely new product or service. But in my experience, the innovation that matters most is usually a small improvement in an established product or service category, executed elegantly.

In other words, find a new way to do something in a well-established market. Creating a new category or market can be incredibly powerful, but it often comes with such a steep education curve that most can't survive long enough to make an impact. Creating products that people should want is a tough way to build a business. On the flip side, creating a new way to look at an existing product or service within a proven market is a strategy that has launched many a successful business. When you keep hearing "nobody does that," you know you're on to something.

Shatto Milk Company (www.shattomilk.com), located on a one-hundred-year-old farm in the rolling hills of northern Missouri, was told more than once: Nobody does that in this industry.

In the mid 1990s the farm could no longer sustain itself, so Leroy Shatto decided save the farm with a bold move. In the traditional dairy model, small farms produce milk and sell it to large co-ops, which either sell it in bulk or package it for large grocery and consumer brands. The farmer is essentially at the mercy of the co-op in terms of both price and practice—the co-op dictates the commodity price, and farmers have no real incentive to produce a higher quality product.

Instead of continuing to participate in the traditional dairy farming model, Shatto started his own brand. Today Shatto Milk is a thriving operation committed to producing milk from cows that are grass-fed and not treated with hormones, bottle the milk themselves in recyclable glass containers, and deliver it from cow to store in around twelve hours, making it the freshest milk available. And "they're" right: Nobody does that.

Be the red leaf

I remember going on a run one chilly late fall morning. As I approached my home, I was struck by the most perfect, vibrant red maple leaf nestled in a large bed of green ivy.

I couldn't help but notice how the contrast made this leaf stand out, and that image has come to signify the way a widely referred business differentiates itself. The market needs a way to distinguish one business from another, and when there is no obvious difference the default measurement will always be price. Can your business be the red leaf?

Anyone who has remodeled a home knows what a long, drawn-out, sometimes unpredictable, and often painful process it can be.

But that's just how it goes, everyone know that, so everyone lives it. Los Angeles remodeling contractor Matt Plaskoff had built a large, thriving remodeling business by 1999 but in an interview he commented that he was frustrated by the lack of systemization and the inability to create a consistent, high-quality result without killing his staff.

"In 2004, he was chosen to lead a project for the television show *Extreme Makeover: Home Edition.* Standing in front of one of the homes that his team had just completed in ONE WEEK, he was asked by one of the producers, 'Can we open a remodeling company that builds really fast and make a living doing it?' Immediately he shared his idea for a concept he called "one week bath," and the producer decided to provide the initial seed capital to begin building the company.

The concept of one week bath is both simple and revolutionary: A customer goes online and designs the bath. The crew shows up and is done in a week. Fast. Efficient. Consistent. Few people in the industry dare to copy his guarantee—on time, on budget, or they pay you. Now that's a red leaf.

There are a handful of ways to discover your innovation:

Study your competition. One of things you will find is that many people in your industry are saying the same things—I think that's the first step in realizing there's an opportunity to step outside the norm. Look at this as your baseline. You may indeed discover a company or two that has captured an innovative approach. There may be room for you to learn from them.

Study difference makers in other industries. What do the brands you already admire do that you don't? If you hire a consultant to help you build your marketing system, look to one who has experience outside of your industry. So often business owners want to work with consultants with expertise in their own industry. While this can make it easier in terms of working with the consultant, it often brings insights that are well-worn in your business. Those outside of your specific industry might be able to give you a fresh perspective.

Talk to your customers. Ask you ideal customers what you do that they value. Chances are it's not what you think; often it's something you need to tap into even more and then communicate as your core talkable difference.

Differences are everywhere waiting for you to claim them. They exist in the way you market your products and services, in the creative packaging of those products and services, in the delivery of those products and services, in narrow market niches, in your processes, and in your people.

I once worked with an architectural firm that, though they thought their strength was their design, heard from one customer after another that it was the way they could cut through city red tape and get a project approved, thereby releasing the first payment to the contractor, that was the real differentiator.

From that lesson they started communicating about how they could help their customers get paid faster as often as they discussed their design skills.

When you find your red leaf and can honestly say you have no direct competition to speak of, you're probably on your way.

The core difference captured

Once you land upon a truly innovative way to stand out, it's essential that you also find a way to capture and communicate the essence of that difference in the simplest way possible. In fact, if the name of your organization can accomplish this task, you've hit a home run. The more you feel the need to explain what makes your organization talkable, the less it probably is.

A name that communicates a metaphor can act as a powerful foundation for your core difference. Business names like ConstantContact (www.constantcontact.com), an e-mail service provider, and Geek Squad (www.geeksquad.com), an on-call, high-tech technical support organization, evoke images of differentiation without the need for much explanation.

You may also find ways to communicate your difference as a mash up or intersection of previously unrelated ideas. This technique is often used in the movie business when someone is trying to get a studio's attention quickly. Prospects will take a well-known hit and tie their movie to it but explain how it's different. For instance, *Speed* might be described as "*Die Hard* on a bus."

Take your innovation, the core talkable difference you want to convey to your market, and create a mash-up phrase: "We're like ___, but with ___."

Visualizing the ideal customer

Not everyone with money is an ideal customer. There are some customers your business should never attempt to appeal to. You need to understand this so that everything you do is directed at those you can provide the greatest results for. Attempting to work with clients who are not ideal is what leads to most of the negative buzz created around a brand.

Here's a test: Whether you install HVAC systems, offer legal services, or create hand-painted greeting cards, at the end of the day your ideal customers should achieve some variation of the same five things:

1. Make money
2. Save time
3. Save energy
4. Save or not lose money today and in the future
5. Feel better about themselves

Make sure you understand what your products and services are going to offer your ideal customer or segments. From this point of view you can begin to describe and define their needs with an eye on categorizing their wants, needs, and behaviors as thoroughly as you might their demographics.

Create a picture in your mind of your ideal customer. Using images of real-life customers can prove an effective way to help everyone in your organization narrowly focus on, and communicate in ways that more directly appeal to, your specific ideal customer. A detailed profile, one that includes photos and stories of real customers, should be part of your marketing strategy documents. You may never share this type of document publicly, but it can be one of the most important internal training documents you ever create.

In order to create your profile you need to understand as much about your ideal customer as possible. Remember the key term here—ideal. I suggest looking long and hard at the characteristics of your most profitable customers that also currently refer business to you—that's the model of an ideal customer.

Once you dig deep and profile the common characteristics, you should also start asking yourself some questions about these folks. Here are some to start with:

- What brings them joy? Is it time with family, reduced stress?
- What are they worried about? Is it money or being cheated?

- What challenges do they face? Stress, fear, or loneliness?
- What do they hope to gain from us? Pride, control, convenience?
- What goals are they striving to attain? Wealth, pleasure, entertainment?
- Where do they get their information? Search engines, friends, peers?
- Who do they trust most? Rabbi, mother-in-law, nobody?

The answers to these types of questions are not always available, but pondering them in relationship to your ideal customer may help you to more fully address their wants and needs in every interaction and communication.

Complete the profile, add a real photo, and hang it up in your office for all to see. Simply hanging photos of your best customers around the office may be the reminder that everyone needs to connect with what your business is really about, what their work is really about, and who really pays everyone's salary.

Here's how an ideal customer description might read for a home remodeling contractor:

> Home owners in five zip codes with an income over $150,000. Married and has owned home for over five years; tend be to entrepreneurs and business owners and know what they want. Have remodeled before and have a deadline or event that dictates completion time. Do a great deal of entertaining and are very active in local community activities. Spends between $50,000 and $150,000 on new kitchens and baths. Intends to stay in home for at least five more years.

For some organizations it can actually be more helpful to start with who is not an ideal customer, whom you cannot or won't serve, who is unable to experience the true value of your products and services in ways that would motivate them to talk about the logical and emotional satisfaction your organization delivers. If you own a hardware store perhaps this would be limited to shoplifters, but if you have a service business this could certainly include a customer that comes to you looking for a reduced price or a customized approach that doesn't fit with your business model or current resources.

The key story

People don't talk about boring products, and they certainly don't talk about boring companies.

A few years ago I had the pleasure of interviewing Tom Szaky, CEO and founder of TerraCycle (www.terracycle.net), a company now considered by many to be one of the leaders in the production of recycled and green products. In fact, TerraCycle is far more than just an eco-conscious company; Szaky has created an entire business model around producing products with zero or even negative production cost. That's right: They produce all of their products from someone else's waste stream, and in some cases make a profit even before they sell the product.

But, it's Szaky's own story that I want to highlight here.

At age nineteen, Szaky and his Princeton college friends were looking for a better way to grow pot. I know, not the most promising start to a marketing story, but stay with me. After some trial and error they landed upon a fertilizer formulated from worm castings—yes, worm poop. The fertilizer worked so well they decided to create a business that produced it for sale.

They entered their business idea in a business plan contest and won a cash prize sufficient to get the operation rolling. They continued to enter and win business plan contests as a form of financing. Meanwhile their very unique product (worm poop fertilizer) started to get noticed by the likes of the *New York Times* and *Inc.* magazine before they actually had a product ready to sell to retailers.

In an effort to save money, Szaky decided to bottle their first batches of liquid plant fertilizer in empty plastic soda bottles, partly because they fit standard-size spray tops and partly because they could go grab them right out of people's recycling bins.

Emptying people's recycling bins landed them in some temporary hot water with the local recycling companies. Eventually they turned to area schools with a "bottle brigade" program in which schools would collect recyclable bottles and give them to TerraCycle and in return TerraCycle would pay the school or organization for collecting the bottles. This built-in community component would later become a key word-of-mouth strategy as they expanded nationally and could tap schools in other communities while gently promoting their consumer products to the school parents.

The decision to rely on recycled waste for production material transformed TerraCycle. Instead of simply producing environmentally friendly, affordable, and effective plant food, they became a company that produced a variety of products made entirely from waste streams. TerraCycle now produces holiday bows from Clif bar wrappers, trash cans from plastic computer cases, pencil cases and backpacks from juice pouches, and kites from Oreo wrappers.

"Waste has historically had a negative value," Szaky told me. "We pay others to take it away. TerraCycle has flipped that notion on its head—we've found a way to turn waste into a valuable asset and a raw material." Today TerraCycle produces dozens of products and generates millions of dollars in revenue from its "upcycling" practices. Szaky is featured as a speaker on business management, innovation, and recycling issues and is the author of *Revolution in a Bottle: How TerraCycle Is Redefining Green Business.*

TerraCycle's story was an essential element that created buzz and led to the company's introduction to the likes of Home Depot before anyone had ever heard of them or had much reason to believe they would be a viable company.

Most talked-about businesses rely on a story that reveals the essence of what they stand for or how they are different. Their core story is compelling, captivating, and easy to retell. It is attractive to customers, attractive to journalists, attractive to suppliers, and attractive to potential employees.

Stories create connection; as Mister Rogers would say, "It's hard not to like someone once you know their story." More than that, stories are vehicles that transport people to their deepest emotional places while conveying the more practical aspects of your business. (Remember, we need to connect logically and emotionally.) Have you ever had an experience in which you heard a compelling story about a business, and without knowing much more you felt unexplainably compelled to support or do business with them?

Every person has a story, every business has a story, and prospects and customers love good stories. People connect with stories that are personal, telling, truthful, and relevant.

So what's your story?

1. Craft a story about you, your company, and your products and services that allows you to convey who you are, why you do what you do, what keeps you awake at night, what motivates, thrills, and scares you, what makes you laugh, what you've chosen to do to make this a better world. Don't give them a chronological history of your company. Instead, talk about the moment you came face-to-face with the biggest, most audacious idea you ever had and charged right in. Talk about what was missing in the world until you created your big idea. Talk about how, even though cleaning windows seems like an unglamorous task to most, you have loved doing it since you were a kid and now you've created a company around that passion.

2. Get your story down to one page and start testing it on people you know—spouses and teenagers are good subjects. Adjust and revise based on the elements that seem to resonate with your test subjects most. Then you need to start living your story and using your story as a core marketing message. Your story, if done well, is the foundation element for what makes you stand out. Use it on your Web site, on the backs of invoices, during sales presentations, and as a hiring tool.

Leader as storyteller

The leader's role in the organization can be that of primary storyteller. The leader creates the story, lives the story, keeps the story alive, and coaches everyone in the organization to tell the story.

It's said that Southwest Airlines (www.southwest.com) founder Herb Kelleher chain-smokes, loves Wild Turkey whiskey, and frequently dresses up as Elvis for company functions. Above all, Kelleher, now officially retired as the company's spokesman, was a legendary story creator and teller. Quite possibly his most famous story surrounded an ongoing battle with a competitor airline in the early days of the company. The story is chronicled in great detail in Kevin and Jackie Freiberg's book *Nuts!*

The story, dubbed "Malice in Dallas," was just a friendly contest between Southwest Airlines, represented by Herb Kelleher, and Stevens Aviation (www.stevensaviation.com), championed by chairman Kurt Herwald, to decide the rights to a slogan. Stevens, an aviation sales and maintenance company in Greensville, South Carolina, had been using "Plane Smart" as its slogan at least one year before Southwest unknowingly began infringing with its "Just Plane Smart" ad campaign. After bringing this to Southwest's attention, Stevens Aviation proposed that, rather than paying teams of lawyers to hash out the dispute over many months and under cover of hundreds of thousands of dollars in fees, the companies send their top warriors to battle it out, one-on-one, in an arm-wrestling tournament before an audience of their employees and the media.

According to the Freibergs, Malice in Dallas is now an epic, a story thousands of people inside and outside Southwest Airlines know almost by heart. This rambunctious alternative to a drawn-out, boring, lawyer-enriching, half-million-dollar courtroom battle was exactly the sort of antic that Americans have come to associate with their favorite maverick airline.

Many businesses have actually reached some level of success based on the founder's ability to tell a fictional story about the business, product, service, or results before they are quite a reality. I wonder how much business has been won on the heartfelt belief that "if they buy it, we'll figure out how to make it."

Great leaders are natural storytellers, but even business owners who would never readily consider themselves to be great leaders often can't help but tell their story so passionately that those who listen simply want to believe.

Referral brand elements

Small-business owners in particular seem to struggle with the idea of "brand," but when it comes to getting people talking about your business, the elements that make up the little things about it are so vitally important. Too often businesses think in terms of names and logos as the only real branding elements they control.

Take a moment to think about your favorite businesses to do business with. What is it that makes them so special? Is it the way they always greet you across the counter, the package the product arrives in, the follow-up thank-you note, the design, the little surprise touches that spell thoughtfulness? Each and every one of these, practiced intentionally or not, is an element of that organization's brand.

Let's return to my example case study for this chapter, sweetriot, for a couple of tangible illustrations of this point.

> **The name**—Sarah tells me she agonized over finding something that felt sweet (ok, duh) but also felt full of the energy that she and her team planned to bring to this space: A sweetriot is a joyful celebration of culture, diversity, and understanding; it is the opposite of a civil riot, which is dangerous, violent, and oppressive.
>
> **The logo**—This one is subtle and, in fact, I missed it for a while. Sweetriot's logo is a thumbprint (it's actually Sarah's sister's thumb) with a globe motif layered over the thumb. This is Sweetriot's way to symbolize their mark on the world
>
> **The product**—Sweetriot's primary products are all-natural, anti-oxidant–rich, dairy-free, kosher, gluten-free dark chocolate cocoa nibs—except, of course, they're called "peaces." I mean, what else would you call them, right?
>
> **The package**—Core products are shipped in stylish tins adorned with artwork from up-and-coming artists. In

addition to the chocolate, the tins contain a fortune. Each quarter sweetriot customers are offered the opportunity to help choose the next featured artist. The tins are recyclable, and sweetriot produces ideas on ways to reuse the tins as well.

The process—Since cacao is generally only found in Latin America, Africa, and Asia, most is imported away to North America and the United States. Sweetriot of course pursued fair trade practices immediately, but wanted to take it a step beyond fair trade, to create not only fair bean pricing and opportunities for farmers, but also for the production of its product in the country the beans came from. There is a new term coming about, "equitrade," meant to capture the idea of trade that is equitable to all parties involved in the process, and Sweetriot uses these principles as another differentiator. Packaging and marketing materials contain stories about the farmers and suppliers in Latin America.

The people—Sweetriot's staff members are called rioters, and the company Web site includes a host of volunteer rioters and rioting gurus—a group of volunteer advisers. The first day of training is called riotation. My guess is that if you sat in on a staff meeting there would be plenty of talk about ways to imprint the attributes of the brand in every tactical discussion.

To some this might just feel like a set of cute touches from a highly creative business owner. But remember: This is a company founded by a Harvard MBA with a few years of high-tech marketing under her belt for good measure. These little touches are intentional flourishes that help amplify the company's message and mission in ways that open doors, excite journalists, and cause people to talk.

Even a branded out-of-office note

So much about small-business branding comes down to paying attention to the smallest details and putting them into the smallest things—like your voice-mail message, fax cover sheet, and even your automated out-of-office e-mail reply.

Andy Sernovitz, author of *Word of Mouth Marketing*, gets this. Instead of sending out the typical "I'm on vacation" message, this made me stop, laugh, and think about Andy's brand. It's always the little stuff!

> I'm off on vacation from Aug. 13-24.
> No, really, I am. For real.
> I'll be camping somewhere, with minimal access to phone and e-mail. If it's an emergency or urgent new business, please send an e-mail and I'll call you from a Starbucks.
> Actually, they recently installed a Starbucks in the trunk of my car, because having a store every 80 yards just wasn't enough.
> Other options:
>
> 1. Take a vacation too.
> 2. Call my office #. It forwards to my cell. I'll check messages on occasion.
> 3. Order a shipment from http://www.corkysbbq.com/
> 4. Procrastinate by writing a silly and long out of office message.
> 5. Find me a new assistant, hire them, then have them call me. (Seriously, I'm hiring a new team, so send resumes.)
> 6. Read the funniest thing ever written: http://www.candyboots.com/wwcards.html
> 7. Buy this album: http://www.amazon.com/Fillmore-East-Frank-Zappa-Mothers/dp/B0000009S9/
>
> Cheers,
> Andy

What intentional flourishes must you add to help amplify your strategy?

The secret sauce: TIHWDIH

There are seven words that the most widely referred businesses use as a way to free themselves and their people to perform in a manner that can provide the customer with the best possible experience. Those words are: "This is how we do it here."

Those words, uttered in many a selling situation, can keep you from promising something you can't deliver or cutting your prices on demand.

Of course, it's not just the words, it's actually following through on them. Every small business is constrained by its ability to deliver the goods with limited resources. The best way to do that is to get very good at a set of proven processes and then stick to them as though your life depended upon it.

Widely referred businesses always have a special way of doing it that plays a key role in attracting and converting the right leads, properly orienting new customers, doing the work and shipping the product, and then following through to make certain a customer is happy.

The first place you might start saying TIHWDIH is during the selling process. When the prospect starts the sales call off with a round of pointed questions and pronouncements of just what it is they need, stop them and suggest that you would like to walk them through a process that you've found can help them uncover the value of working together, or not, head-on and that you would like to engage them in that process. (That's code for TIHWDIH.)

I'm not saying that there is never a time to bend and flex as new opportunities arise. Rather, that without your own stated processes for excellence you will get pushed and shoved more than bent and flexed. Sticking with your proven delivery mechanisms will help you avoid taking business that you know you shouldn't take. Your processes are the filter for identifying ideal customers. (If a prospect won't sit still for your needs analysis, that might be a red flag.)

For example, in a consulting environment, it's generally a good idea to state very clearly up front the level of participation the client must commit to, the documents and reports you'll need access to, and how the flow of meetings and communication should work. If a client waffles here, things will go downhill fast.

I've worked with software programmers who tell me it's commonplace in their industry for projects to never be completed because a business-development person is so eager to get the business that the scope of the project is never nailed down. This can apply to window cleaners, plumbers, and remodelers as well. Too often a prospect wants you to jump in your truck and come out and bid a job just so they can find the lowest price. This is fine, but you're not the lowest price, you do special work, carry proper insurance and licenses, and pay your people well. A sales process that stops the customer long enough to appreciate those differences is essential. This approach won't appeal to every potential customer, but you're not looking for every potential customer; you're looking for ideal customers who appreciate the extra care and attention you bring to every project.

Your processes will ensure that everyone in the organization is delivering the same message, experience, and brand. Remember this: A seemingly great opportunity that pushes you outside of your proven processes often costs far more to deliver, and may even cause you to take you eye off of serving your core ideal customer.

Demonstrating that you actually have proven processes can be very alluring to prospects. Too many small businesses pitching their wares these days are making promises right and left but falling down when it actually comes to delivering on those promises. Your ten-step needs discovery process will automatically set you apart from the pack and will likely lead to the ability to raise your prices.

All of these processes, or touch points, exist as intentional ways to assure customer satisfaction for the widely referred business, but there's always some secret sauce that really makes them stand out.

What's the one way you do business, package your products and services, engage customers, audit for problems, or create a path to the final results about which you can confidently state, "This is how we do it here."

The technology of delegation

Small-business owners really are lousy at delegation (and I'm as guilty of this as you are).

You know nobody can do it like you do; it takes more time to explain it properly than to just do it. And, frankly, it's the work you enjoy; it's where you get the greatest satisfaction, and you can't really let go of it, because what will happen then? And yet, something truly magical will happen in your business when you finally realize you must delegate most of what you do today.

Growth requires delegation (not to be confused with abdication). Delegation requires systems and processes. Getting all the successful ways you do what you do documented can seem like a monumental task if taken on as a grand project one day. The key to delegation and systems thinking is to employ technology married to a checklist mentality.

What I'm really talking about is an operations manual and a set of processes that anyone, perhaps a virtual anyone, can follow. Now don't freeze up at the suggestion of a manual. Think simple baby steps first.

Wikis. A piece of software called a "wiki" is a virtual scratch pad. This online tool will allow you to organize and document everything that you do. Here's the cool thing, though: Anyone in your organization can edit and update any document on your wiki. As long as you can scratch out a few action steps, your team, or even your virtual assistant, may very well be able to finish and refine your processes.

I use a tool called Central Desktop for this, although there are many other low-cost and free options, such as PBworks (pbworks.com) and Google Sites (sites.google.com). This tool allows me to create work spaces—essentially intranets—to which I can grant access to various groups for collaboration purposes. So now, to explain something that I need done, I jot the steps down and capture them in this sortable, searchable operations manual.

Few things are as empowering as documented routine work. When someone can reference a set of documented work steps, they are much freer to focus on the creative elements of their jobs.

E-mail management. E-mail has caused some real problems in business. It's hard to manage, track, sort, respond to, and delegate. A new kind of technology is available that allows you to create mailboxes for sales, service, questions, joint venture offers, quotes, speaking requests, etc., and then build response routines that delegate relevant tasks to people in your organization.

I use E-mail Center Pro from Palo Alto Software to help manage e-mail follow-up and delegation. I can assign tasks, view responses, and filter requests from a dashboard. The best part about this is that even with the flood of e-mail we receive, I can see that nothing gets lost. This is far more powerful from a marketing standpoint than help desk software, as it allows us to delegate but still respond as humans to every type of request, even when some of the staff is on vacation.

Open book management

In 1982, International Harvester sent a young manager named Jack Stack to Springfield, Missouri, to fix their ailing engine-overhaul plant. Shortly, International Harvester decided to pull the plug on the plant and ordered Stack and his team to lay off the entire staff. Instead, in what has now become a much chronicled story, Stack and twelve of his fellow managers pulled together $100,000 and borrowed $9 million more to buy the place, renaming it Springfield ReManufacturing Company, or SRC.

I've interviewed Stack on several occasions, and he readily admits that, given the size of the loan payment and the inexperience of the staff, including himself, he decided to open the books as a way to get everyone in the company focused on the financials, so that all the employees could help the company make money and survive.

To him, traditional closed-book management strategies, the kind he experienced rising from mail room to shop floor to management, didn't make any sense, because the reason behind budgets and quotas, profits and losses were never explained. So he and his managers decided to create an entire business where everyone knew everything behind the numbers and everyone was expected to find ways to contribute to the numbers. With that decision, the concept known as "open book management" was born.

SRC's and Stack's complete story can be found in a wonderful book by Stack and coauthor Bo Burlingham known as *The Great Game of Business*. Burlingham covered SRC and the great game as a columnist for *Inc.* magazine. "Stack had figured out how to tap into the most underutilized resource available to a company," Burlingham wrote. "Namely, the intelligence of the people who work for it."

Open book management fits perfectly with the concept of employees as customers and, again in the words of Burlingham, "I met fuel-injection-pump rebuilders who knew the gross margins of every nozzle and pump they produced. I met crankshaft grinders and engine assemblers who could discuss the ROI of their machine tools. I met a guy who worked on turbochargers and ran his area as if it were his own small business. Then again, why shouldn't he? Like the other employees, he was an owner of SRC."

Stack turned his ideas and model into SRC Holdings Corp., with twenty-two different subsidiaries that employ twelve hundred people and generate combined annual revenue of $230 million.

An *Inc.* magazine survey last year found that 40 percent of the companies on its list of the five hundred fastest-growing private companies in the nation use some form of open book management. There is a misconception in some circles that open book management is simply about sharing the full financial picture with every employee. While some firms may choose to provide full financial details, the real power of any open book management strategy is in giving employees the key measures of business success and teaching them to understand those measures and to use them to improve their performance. It's about fully engaging employees by helping them understand how their specific function plays a role in the overall success of the organization. It's about, as Stack chose to paint it, making business a game and teaching everyone the rules—how to keep to score, and how to win.

I find that many business owners aren't that hot at tracking and measuring the important indicators of success. When you are just starting out, perhaps you can get away with this, but as your business grows, analyzing key success indicators can mean the difference between smart growth and chaos. Most of the books on the subject of business or marketing metrics are so full of jargon that they don't provide anything in the way of a simple and effective approach. I firmly believe that if you mine your data for just a handful of key indicators, you can create a dashboard of information that you can actually react to, affect, and lead from. Keep it simple and build elegant processes to extract and monitor just a handful of key indicators.

From a financial health standpoint, cash flow and profit are the two most important to understand, and beyond that most growth objectives can be measured against these four goals:

Lead generation. Where do the best leads come from? How many do you need to generate, and what actually generates them? If you don't know this, it's likely you will waste lots of money on things that are generating the wrong kinds of leads or, potentially worse, abandon a lead-generation tactic that's actually working. Of course, this means that you must be tracking what leads convert to customers and which customers are most profitable.

Percentage of leads converted. The biggest resource-killer of all businesses is the chasing of leads that are not qualified, not educated (by you, not in life), and not ready to appreciate the unique value your organization has to offer. When you start to measure this and discover, as so many organizations do, that they are converting a very low number of leads, you'll have to fix it. It's too painful otherwise.

Cost per customer acquisition. Every new customer comes with a cost. By marrying that cost with some sort of value to the organization over time, you have a metric that can determine what you can actually afford to spend to acquire a new customer and go to work on lowering that cost while creating more accurate budget forecasts.

Average dollar transaction per customer. It's generally much easier to increase your revenue through additional sales to existing customers than to go out and find new ones. You can do this one of two ways: increase the perceived value of your offerings and raise your prices or consider supplementing your core offering with products and services that meet additional needs.

As you can see, no rocket science with this list, but tell me, are you really measuring these four significant numbers? So often business owners and managers get caught up in trying to track so many metrics that it's nearly impossible to focus on what's truly significant.

So what's there to gain by focusing on these particular indicators?

Tripling or quadrupling your lead-conversion number is usually the easiest thing to do once you start paying attention to it. It's much harder, however, to significantly increase the number of leads. But through careful lead analysis you can cut the cost per lead greatly by making better lead spending decisions.

By creating a cost-per-new-customer baseline, you can begin to budget and plan growth much more accurately than ever before. In fact, this is where you can come full circle with your marketing measurement, because now when the CEO (or you) suggests that the marketing plan calls for 25 percent growth over the next eighteen months, you can begin to tie specific marketing and sales activities and spends to achieving that result—or at least to demonstrating why it's not realistic.

Staff: Blocking and tackling

It's not enough for the CEO or head of marketing to understand and create the various strategic elements discussed throughout this chapter, including the financial and market metrics just discussed. You must also teach these elements as the fundamental building blocks of your employee training. Stack refers in *The Great Game of Business* to this practice as "huddles," and I think the continued use of the sports metaphor is appropriate.

Larry Bird, one of basketball's all-time greats, was legendary for shooting hundreds of free throws every day. He was the league MVP four times and led the NBA in free-throw percentage each of the four years he was honored.

Ask yourself what fundamental marketing "drills" you, and everyone in the organization, should be doing on at least a weekly basis to become marketing MVPs? (Or at least to get off the bench.)

Here are some suggestions for starters:

- Review and discuss progress versus goals on all key strategic and financial goals
- Review a description and perhaps even photos of the ideal customer
- Review a list of trigger phrases customers say out loud or to themselves when expressing a need for what you sell
- Review and practice answering this question in a marketing way: What do you do for living? Sample answer: "I help contractors get paid faster" instead of "I'm an architect"
- Review and practice the most effective way to describe the value your organization brings in thirty seconds or less
- Answer at least one phone or written customer/prospect inquiry, no matter your job title
- Call one customer and ask them to share something they need, want, like, or dislike about doing business with your organization
- Review a list of stated organizational or personal marketing goals and the indicators used to track them.

So what do your organization's layups and free throws look like, and have you done yours today?

Your strategy action plan

I know there was a lot in this chapter, so before we move on let's recap and create a list of action steps to think about while creating your authentic strategy.

The higher purpose—Can you identify a sense of mission that ultimately drives why your organization does what it does? Not the standard-issue mission statement—a goal or purpose that everyone's passionate about.

Nobody does that—What is the talkable innovation that you are going push out into the market as a clear demonstration of your unique way of doing business?

The core difference captured—What simple phrase, metaphor, or slogan can you create to simplify and quickly communicate what your core difference is?

Visualizing the ideal customer—Can you formulate precisely what your ideal customer looks like?

The key story—What is the simple truth contained in your primary marketing story? Can you can utilize this story to help illustrate what makes your organization unique?

Leader as storyteller—How can you teach and keep the story as an integral part of your organization's culture?

Referral brand elements—What imagery, identity elements, processes, and small flourishes will you use to further communicate the essential differentiation and core marketing message?

The secret sauce: TIHWDIH—What unique process of approach to doing business is going to act as the lever for delivery on your key point of differentiation?

The technology of delegation—What tools will you use to empower everyone in the organization to collaborate in the success of the customer experience?

Open book management—What set of numbers and key indicators do you need to track and teach in order to help everyone in the organization understand how the business grows?

Staff: blocking and tackling—What exercises, scorecards, and processes do you need to create and utilize to keep the elements of your authentic strategy top of mind and evolving with the entire staff?

Customer success quotient—Create the indicators and processes needed to capture the ultimate measure of marketing success—customer results.

CHAPTER 6

Content as Marketing Driver

I n this chapter we will cover the many facets of creating education-based marketing messages and content that create awareness and attract good leads. Your charge, although it may feel a bit daunting by the time you finish this chapter, will be to create a toolbox of information that can be used by your organization as well as your customers and strategic partners (direct and indirect networks) to properly educate and inform prospects.

Traditional lead-generation tactics like directory advertising, trade show participation, and half-page print ads are quickly losing appeal with small-business marketers. There are two very good reasons for this decline: (1) traditional methods are some of the most expensive, and (2) traditional methods are proving less effective than newer alternatives.

Message and information overload, technology to block ads such as caller ID, TiVo, spam filtering, ad blockers, do-not-call lists, commercial-free satellite radio, and the availability of vast amounts of information online may make traditional and more expensive outbound marketing efforts a thing of the past. This trend will only continue to get stronger. Generation Y and its younger counterparts no longer rely on the Yellow Pages, don't read newspapers, and watch TV like an interactive sport (when not playing Wii or watching commercial-free TV online).

Small businesses must change the way they think about and

approach lead generation. They must think in terms of being found instead of finding. People are still looking for solutions, trying out new services, and buying things they want; they've just changed how they go about doing it.

Technology put the phone directory in our pockets, removed the need for trade shows because of the ease of placing interactive demos online, and provided us with all the product information and reviews we could ever consume in the form of blogs, search engines, and social media sites.

So in order to generate leads and be found you must put yourself in the path of people who are learning about and shopping in your industry. You must create a total Web presence for your business and then create spokes, online and off-line, that lead people to your hub.

The beauty of this approach is that once you master it, the leads and referrals you turn up will be of a much higher value, more qualified and likely expecting to pay a premium because they have, through the consumption of your education-based marketing materials and content, convinced themselves that your products and services hold the answer to their particular needs.

Don't get me wrong here: I'm not saying that all lead generation must be done exclusively online, and I'm not saying to skip advertising. What I am saying is that your online presence should be the hub of your brand, and that your online and off-line advertising, PR, and referral systems should take advantage of these tools to their fullest.

Once again, think of it as lighting candles along dark paths so that weary travelers can discover you in the dark.

Those candles are your education-based entries in social media sites like Twitter and Facebook—gentle guides of introduction. They are your white papers and free reports that teach prospects that you have the required expertise and experience. They are your PR efforts and articles, written to illuminate your expertise. They are your blog posts, designed to attract surfers looking for the way. They are your strategic partnerships, alignments that evoke trust. They are your Web conferences, providing interactive discussions with customers and prospects. They are your community-building events, places where candles can be relit and shared.

You can no longer sit back, dump an offer in the mail, and start working the phones; you've got to build your inbound marketing machine and start taking advantage of the power of information, networking, trust, connection, and community to generate leads.

As we turn our attention to this education-based, inbound approach, keep in mind this very important reason for going to this trouble: An educated customer will always be a better customer. You should spend a great deal of time attracting the ideal customer, and one of the best ways to do that is to make sure they know who they are. You do that by teaching them how you work, how your approach gets results, what you expect of them, and why, perhaps, your products and services are more or less expensive than others.

Syms Clothing (www.syms.com), a New York discount men's clothing store, has famously used "an educated consumer is our best customer" for years to assert that educated shoppers were less willing to support the high markups and expenses of conventional retailers. Do all of the above and you will discover that selling gets easier, and doing the work with happy, motivated customers gets everyone the results they are looking for.

Your killer "Technology"

The word technology is in quotes in this heading because I need to expand your view of how it's used here. Widely referred businesses, ones that get talked about, do something different. We've talked about the idea of being different at length, but we need to bring that difference to the forefront of all marketing communications by developing tools that promote your point of view, your secret way of doing things, your core difference. It's not enough to say how you're different; you've also got to develop tools and materials that illustrate that difference as well.

So in that vein, your technology could be a seven-step approach, a discovery audit, an actual technological product advancement, a coaching process, a set of tools, or proprietary software. The key is to capture what it is that you do that's unique and valuable and expand it into something you can build a great deal of your educational content platform around. Think of this as your organization's signature tool.

When I created the Duct Tape Marketing System I knew that one of my objectives was to make marketing simple while still getting business owners to understand the essential elements. We boiled our entire process down to seven steps and created a white paper and presentation called "The Seven Steps to Small Business Marketing Success." That title has been downloaded hundreds of thousands of times, been presented to tens of thousands of small business owners in person live and online, and acts as the central lead-conversion presentation for Duct Tape Marketing coaches around the world.

The seven steps are our technology and are central to our core message of simple, effective, and affordable small-business marketing. Each of the steps of course can be expanded to fill up the space of a stand-alone white paper or presentation as well, making this technology a dynamic and flexible source of content.

Every business needs to create or capture their simple strategy, differentiator, or process that allows them to communicate their unique difference in thirty seconds or less. But once you've gained attention, you also need a tool that allows you to expand the workings of your killer technology in more detailed terms. You need to be able to effectively expand your thirty-second version to a thirty-minute one that you might give as a sales presentation or use as the basis for an educational workshop.

Then you can create multiple versions on the same theme to keep it interesting and varied for different audiences. For instance, you can have the "7 Steps to Get a Result You Want" version and then the "7 Things You Must Avoid to Get a Result you Want" version.

In my experience it's the business that takes the time and effort to document their special approach that is seen as a more credible expert on whatever topic they are addressing, is able to more easily explain their unique approach, and can open up more channels to spread their message through speaking, cobranding, and joint ventures.

Point-of-view white paper

Once you create, capture, organize, or otherwise formulate your big technology, you've got to get to work creating the documents and processes that will bring it to life in the minds of your customers and prospects. To begin, create your point-of-view white paper.

Now, before you conjure up images of page after page of boring, technical specs, the stuff of the traditional white paper, know that I only use that term because it's widely accepted. Also know that Referral Engine businesses don't tolerate boring, so I'm really talking about your "white-hot paper." This is the primary tool your use to educate prospects, partners, and other collaborators, and it can be as fun, campy, gorgeous, technical, or creative as you need it to be to align with your strategy of difference from the last chapter. One way or the other, it's going to be a workhorse. There are two resources I recommend on this subject: *The White Paper Marketing Handbook* by Bob Bly and Michael Stelzner's *Writing White Papers*. Reading these books is the best way to get a total education on the subject.

Beyond your core white paper, there can be e-books, free reports, how-to guides, case studies, tip sheets, trend reports, and more. Eventually you will get so used to this idea of education-based marketing and inbound lead generation that you will start to look for ways to create all of the above and publish and republish in multiple formats and mediums.

But for now, back to our point-of-view white paper.

This is something that could easily function as an overall strategy document for your business, much like the seven steps point of view does for my business. It is a document that has a very long shelf life and can act as a business generator now and far into the future. It is the primary tool that your referral sources can employ to easily demonstrate why they are referring your business and, because it's a tangible piece of education and not hype or pure fluff, it's something prospects can return to as they progress in their own sales timeline.

What goes in it?

You should give your white paper a name that screams benefit to the reader. Just like titles of books and headlines in ads, the title of your white paper should be something that really grabs a prospect's attention and makes them want to take a peek.

Create a short summary of what the reader will get from reading the white paper. Sprinkle in stories and quotes from real customers. Use lots of relevant images, charts, graphs, and detailed statistics to back any claims you make.

Finally, end with a call to action and a description of how your firm might help the reader take the next step. Don't blow the point of the education process by coming on too strong, but if someone has made it to the end of your twenty-page or even five-page document, they might readily welcome some advice on how they can put what they've just read into action.

The E-myth: Why Most Small Businesses Don't Work and What to Do About It, written by Michael Gerber, is a wonderful book that addresses how to build a business that works. But, it's also the basis of a consulting practice delivered by E-Myth Worldwide (www.e-myth .com). One of the core components of E-Myth is something they call the E-myth Point of View—a foundation of five core principles that the entire consulting and coaching practice, and its products, are built on. Anyone that visits the E-Myth site can find a number of documents that orient them to this point of view while gently suggesting there are a number ways to acquire the tools and knowledge to implement their system.

In addition to the great content, make certain that it is very easy for a reader to contact you or take the next action, and encourage and facilitate the reader's ability to pass your white paper on to others.

Great content gets you past the gatekeepers

Hopefully the idea of creating valuable content for your inbound marketing effort has captured your imagination by this point. If not, let me give you another perspective.

Content that addresses the concerns of the CEO will get your message past the purchasing agent's filtering system.

Let me explain. You're selling your solutions to XYZ Corporation, and Bob, the director of purchasing, isn't returning your phone calls. Then, one day, Susan, the CEO, bursts into Bob's office and says she wants the entire sales team to attend a presentation called "How to Get

Sales and Marketing on the Same Team." It just so happens that you're presenting this killer workshop, one that addresses the very thing that keeps Susan up at night.

Oh, and Bob's on line two.

By creating marketing materials focused on every level of a prospect's buying chain, you can take much more control over the sales process. CEOs are searching for answers, VPs are searching for answers, and interns are searching for answers. By writing blog posts, creating white papers, and offering Web conferences that address the needs and concerns of all three, you can move past the gatekeepers and make the sale. Just another form of inbound lead generation!

For many organizations, getting invited to the table is the most difficult task. Educational content minimizes the need for selling. Content draws leads to you and allows them to find your products and services and sell themselves. My advice is to start your killer point-of-view white paper with an eye toward turning it into a seminar that is totally focused on something your prospects need—make it a topic that is full of valuable information and that will get people's attention.

From this one seminar you can create many of the items listed above and form an on-message, gate-keeper-busting, integrated content strategy.

Hold a testimonial-gathering party

People can be very motivated by the comments of their peers. Gathering and using authentic customer testimonials is a great way to (a) get closer to your customers, and (b) offer proof that your company delivers. I often find that while most business owners understand the power of testimonials, they don't always know the best way to acquire them. All of your educational marketing materials, including your point-of-view white paper, can benefit from third-party endorsements in the form of testimonial comments from happy customers.

So here's an idea that I think works on a number of levels.

Why not create an event around gathering testimonials? Invite your best customers for a networking happy hour. Promote the event as a chance to network, swap stories, and star in the creation of new marketing materials for your company.

Hire a videographer and a photographer, and then, throughout the course of the evening, let your customers cycle through the video seat to tell their story of success with your firm. Most people enjoy being on camera once they do it, and the whole group will be entertained by the event and feed off of each other's energy. Capturing your client success stories and testimonials is something you should be doing anyway, so why not do it all at one time?

You could also apply this tactic during a trade show or other event attended by your customers, particularly if your customers are scattered geographically, making a party less feasible.

Another way to motivate your customers to participate is to offer them the opportunity to create a quick video overview of their own company while at the event, one they can use in their own marketing efforts.

Once you capture video, audio, and still photos from the event, you've got a testimonial and success story library that could infuse your marketing materials, broadcast, and print ads for years. And you've created a customer loyalty and community-building event that may just become next year's hottest party to crash!

What really triggers a referral

Referrals happen most naturally when two people are talking and one of the parties expresses their current pain in the neck. If the other party just had her pain in the neck fixed, she may very well say something like, "You have just gotta call Bob, he's the best pain-in-the-neck fixer on the planet."

Right? We've all had some variation of that exchange in making or receiving a referral.

Problem is, we don't spend enough time teaching our customers and sources the kinds of complaints, frustrations, challenges, and situations that qualify someone as a great referral. Here's what I mean: We ask our customers and referral sources if they know anyone who needs a fully optimized, solutions-driven lawn manicure specialist when we should probably be asking them if they know anyone whose dog keeps getting loose because their lawn service forgets to close the gate.

I believe any salesperson worth their salt has developed a list of phrases, situations, and verbal clues that, if heard during a sales presentation, signal it's time to take the order.

The same idea is true of a qualified referral.

My belief is that the best way to make it easy for people to refer business your way is to develop a list of "trigger" phrases that experience tells you are the exact words your prospects utter when then need what you've got.

For example, if you sell accounting software, it's rare that a prospect might walk up to a golf buddy and say, "I sure wish I had some better accounting software." But he might say, "I have no idea how healthy my business is, because we never have timely data" or "I feel like I'm being help hostage by my accounting firm" or "We keep everything on spreadsheets, and it's a real hassle to update." In many cases these folks don't have any idea that your accounting software is the answer, but you do, so these utterances are your invitation to save the day.

Spend a couple of hours brainstorming with anyone in your organization who has customer contact of any kind, or call up a dozen customers and ask them to identify the true value your firm brings them, with the goal of creating a top ten list of trigger phrases that everyone in your organization and anyone wishing to refer business to you could use as the perfect way to spot your ideal customer. You can use the resulting list in your marketing education process. You can even take it a step further and publicize this content in some manner in your marketing materials, because it's likely that a prospect might be saying these exact things to themselves as well. (This might end up being the best internal sales training tool you've created to date.) You should use this tool with your customers and strategic partners as a way to help them understand how and when to make a referral.

You can close the loop on this process by creating tools like gift certificates, special referral offers, or coupons that your referral sources can use any time they hear a trigger phrase.

Prospect: "I've been waiting over a week for my lawyer to call me back."

Referral Source: "Really? My attorney calls me back within twenty-four hours guaranteed—here's her card. Because I recommended you, she'll review your first contract for free."

Content is the most trusted form of advertising

With the precipitous fall of advertising in the mainstream media, some are starting to wonder publicly if advertising has once and for all run its course as an effective marketing vehicle. But advertising still works, always has and always will. What's changed, however, is that now good advertising works much better than bad advertising. I know that may sound silly, but back in the day when you had one paper and three broadcast TV stations, bad advertising worked pretty well, and that's what got the mainstream media and some advertisers in trouble today.

Now that consumers have unlimited ways to consume content and be entertained, they have an equal number of ways to tune out ads that do nothing more than interrupt them from going where they are headed. That, and the fact that online advertising, an industry that didn't exist twenty years ago, is now a $25 billion business, is why mainstream advertising vehicles are scuffling. Advertising does still work very well; it just works in different ways. Adapt, innovate, and integrate and advertising can still be a killer component in your lead-generation plans.

Today's smart advertiser understands that advertising is less effective at creating sales but very effective at creating awareness, particularly awareness of educational, trust-building content such as your point-of-view white paper. Your advertising's call to action should be one of permission—permission to teach. Effective online ads, once designed solely to attempt to divert attention away from content, have morphed into dynamically generated editorial content. The most successful ads are those that engage a viewer with an offer of valuable content from a trusted resource. Sending a prospect to get content that addresses a specific problem or want is the most logical way to allow them to sell themselves on your eventual solution.

Without the effective use of advertising to light the way to useful content, a great deal of it would never be created or found. That's advertising's true value. When a sales pitch might not be trusted, an educational content campaign might be.

Another form of content advertising (I'm expanding the classic term, but I personally think it applies) is growing daily on sites such as Twitter, LinkedIn, and Facebook. Through careful participation, marketers are growing networks, creating awareness, and eventually driving traffic to their content and their profit-making initiatives. When Brian Clark (@copyblogger) tweets, "Check out today's Landing Page Makeover Clinic at Copyblogger" with a link to his site, is this not an ad? Which is not to disparage it—Clark has earned the right with his followers to draw them to his new content.

Use your advertising to start conversations and draw people into content that builds trust and community, and you'll harness the ever-effective power of advertising for generating leads and sales.

Using online ads for content awareness

Ads on platforms like Facebook have been around for a while now and, based on reviews coming out from some users, the results are mixed. I personally find them to be an effective and intriguing option for many small businesses. Here's why.

You have a very large universe on Facebook, but you can target your ad based on the location, sex, age, education, and keyword interests of its users, making this a potentially narrow ad buy, particularly for a local business. If you want to show your ad to business-type folks only in Denver, Colorado, so be it.

Some detractors claim that Facebook ads don't convert to sales, but I would suggest that this is the wrong way to think about and use this tool. Think of your Facebook ads, or ads in any social media space, as content that is intended to create further awareness about you. See, Facebook ads don't have to link out to your sales page; they can be associated with content right there on Facebook. For instance, if you use the events application to promote an event you are hosting, such as a webinar, you can associate ads with that event and drive targeted people to find out about or even directly RSVP to your event on Facebook. Same is true for the video application.

Use Facebook ads to drive people to a video on Facebook that gives great content and invites them to learn more at your primary Web hub. You can also tightly integrate your ad campaigns with business pages to create outposts for your fan pages and invite narrowly defined target audiences to become a fan on Facebook.

When you use these internal ad plays, your ads, complete with social features, become more like tiny bites of content, instead of sales pitches, and help prospective customers get to know, like, and trust you a bit more before you ever ask for business.

Facebook allows you to buy your ads on a cost-per-click or cost-per-thousand-impressions basis and provides decent real-time reporting, so you can adjust your ads as needed. For a much deeper dive into the ever evolving world of Facebook consider All Facebook (www.allfacebook.com) and Mari Smith's Why Facebook (whyfacebook.com).

PR for buzz

PR, and by that I mean positive mentions of your people, story, products, services, and activities in the media consumed by your ideal target market, is a woefully underutilized tool for lead and referral generation.

There's simply no denying the impact that a third-party endorsement in the press can have on awareness and trust building. As stated early on in this book, widely referred businesses often thrive on a culture of buzz, and positive press is a real buzz catalyst. It's essential to integrate buzz-building routines into your lead-generation plans.

Another often overlooked benefit of positive media coverage is that in addition to creating awareness for your lead generation efforts, it helps to reconfirm the confidence of your existing customers and strategic partners and provides them with tangible proof positive when they move to make a referral.

The proper way to stalk a journalist

One of the keys to creating buzz through PR is to look at the journalists who could potentially spread the word about your organization as a target market—you need them to get to know, like, and trust you just like you would a customer.

Now, would you send a customer a one-page flyer and then follow up with a phone call asking them when they planned to write a story about your company, er, buy from you? No, of course not.

Here's how you get journalists on your side:

- Build a list of journalists who you think might care about your story.
- Read everything they write (use a Google News search by their name and subscribe to their e-mail alerts or RSS feeds—you can follow a lot of journalists this way).
- Find and follow them on Twitter or other social networks.
- Discover their blogs or online columns and subscribe to, comment on, and write relevant trackbacks to it (almost every journalist also writes a blog).
- Set up a routine of sending relevant content to them that is related to articles they write.
- Don't push for any stories (unless they are truly news) until you've done this for weeks.

Here's the thing: If you can prove yourself to be a reliable resource for a journalist, you will be looked upon as a friend. Until then, you're just a pest to an overworked and often underpaid reporter. Understand that journalists need sources, the more credible the better. Prove yourself both articulate and credible, and you will start to create the kind of buzz in the media that makes you very easy to refer.

By following what a journalist writes, you will often find clues to the kinds of things they really care about, how you might pitch them, and what they might write about in the future. I once read an article by *BusinessWeek* columnist Jon Fine. The article was about his initial impressions of using Facebook. I immediately reached out and connected with him through Facebook, and the next thing you knew I had scheduled an interview with him for my podcast. My guess is that if I hadn't been paying attention to what he was writing about, he probably would have ignored my e-mail.

So it takes a little work to earn media mentions, but it can be well worth the time spent.

PR source as a referral tool

Once you get good at understanding the needs of the journalists you build relationships with, you can start to look outside of your own business. No matter what your business does, helping your customers get a story or interview with a journalist will always score you points.

What if you also looked for ways to refer your customers or strategic partners to journalists in need of a good source? What if you taught some of your best customers and strategic partners the six-step routine I've just shared with you? You don't even have to dig through lists of journalists for industry opportunities related to customers' businesses. You can subscribe to a service like Help a Reporter Out (helpareporter .com). This service, founded by PR professional Peter Shankman, matches journalists researching a story with expert sources. Anyone can sign up on the site, which distributes three daily e-mails full of stories just waiting for you to contribute to.

All you need to turn HARO into a referral tool is to read the daily e-mails with two hats on. One, look for stories you could add to, and two, scan through the queries thinking about any of your customers, partners, suppliers, or prospects who could be offered up as resources to a journalist. If you take five minutes a day sending off appropriate story ideas to your network, the referral tap will open in your direction in a matter of a few short weeks.

Remember, referrals are about trust and relationship building, and nothing does that faster than showing someone that you are committed to finding ways to help them get what they need to succeed.

Speaking for leads and buzz

Earlier I suggested that you should harness your signature technology and expand the description into a point-of-view white paper. The next logical step in my mind is to create one or more presentations from this effort that can be delivered live, in person or via Web conference. By developing a series of educational talks or workshops, you can immediately gain access to groups of prospects hungry for your great how-to advice.

Understand that I'm not talking about warmed-over sales presentations. I'm talking about developing presentations that teach people how to do something, even if that something isn't directly related to your business or product or if you're showing potential customers how to do what you do by themselves.

Few things say expert louder than a group inviting you to present information on a hot topic. It's certainly great if a topic you are asked to present ties directly to your core products, but many times you can get even greater benefit simply by sharing useful information. In some circles this makes you even more attractive, as it's obvious you are not just trying to pitch for sales.

For example, let's say your organization sells lines of commercial insurance and you've discovered a very effective way to find, train, and retain top salespeople. Creating a presentation called something like "Secrets to Finding, Training, and Retaining Top Producers" would make you a sought-after speaker for many groups. Well, guess who you might find in the audience for a presentation like that? Prospects, customers, potential strategic partners, and even top producers.

Getting up in front of audiences large and small is not just an efficient way to get exposure and build trust; it's integral to raising your status as an adviser and expert. Widely referred businesses always look for ways to participate in conferences, provide great workshops for associations, and schedule Web conferences as part of their overall marketing package.

Here are some tips to keep in mind to make your speaking pay off big.

Get referred—You can create your own workshop events, but one of my favorite strategies is to approach two potential groups and offer to present great information to their clients and networks. The key here is that you have a topic that is very hot and seen as very valuable. This is not a sales presentation; it's an educational and value-added tool. Approach your two partners with the idea that you'll present a great topic, they offer it to their customers, and they get to cross-promote to each other's attendees as part of the deal. You simply get referred in as the expert. (Every time you do this you will be asked to speak at an event one of the attendees is involved with as well.)

Make a deal with the sponsor—You are a highly sought after speaker willing to waive your fee only if they permit you to elegantly reveal that there is a way for attendees to acquire your products and services, and that you will also be offering some free stuff in exchange for the contact information of those interested in the free stuff. Make it known that you have no intention of selling, merely informing. This approach raises the value of your presentation and gets you what you need: a lead-generation opportunity. This can be a deal breaker for you or the sponsor. If you over promote, don't expect to get asked back; if they won't allow you to acquire leads, don't bother.

Educate like crazy—Don't be afraid to give away all of your secrets. Some folks suggest you should just tell them what they need but not how to get it done. I don't agree. If you tell them how, some may think they can do it themselves, but those who really want what you have will realize through your specific details, how-tos, and examples that you do indeed possess the knowledge and tools to help them get what they want. Educate, and you won't have to sell!

Collect those addresses—In some cases people will rush up to you after a thought-provoking presentation and ask how they can buy, but, in case they don't, make sure you give all attendees a valuable reason to share their contact information for the purpose of follow-up. You can offer them the slides to your presentation, a free resource guide related to your topic, or a more detailed report based on the topic in exchange for business cards. If you don't have this preplanned, you'll find you won't get a second chance to wow these folks. Of course, I hope it goes without saying that you should also have a follow-up process. Send a handwritten note, add them into a pre-written "drip" e-mail campaign on the topic, or call them up after the event to measure their engagement.

Simple call to action—When I first starting speaking in the manner I've described here, I would pour my heart out, mindful of not selling, and then come to the end, and there would be this awkward moment when I knew people wanted to buy something but I didn't have an offer. Well, I quickly learned that that didn't serve either of us very well. If you provide great information and a clear road map to solve someone's problems, you'll often find them wanting you to reveal how they could take the next step. But here's the key: In that environment they want a special deal as an incentive for acting right now. Not every audience or speaking engagement will present this opportunity, but I've found that in a nonpaid speaking gig, where I've been given permission to introduce my products and services, this three-step approach is well received.

1. Tell your audience right up front that you're going to give them great information, and tell them at the end about what you do.

2. About halfway through, after you've built some trust, take a quick minute to reveal, for instance, a paid workshop or program you have coming up, tell them the price, and go on.

3. At the end, answer questions, make free offers, and, almost as an afterthought, agree to let them also bring a friend to the event you mentioned at the same price if they sign up today. (You've just made the event half price in their minds, turned them into recruiters, and given your potential attendees a valuable tool to offer to a friend or colleague.)

So all of a sudden, anyone considering the offer is now highly motivated by this compelling change of events. Don't hard sell this; simply put it out there and let people do the math. Don't risk tainting your wonderful information with a sales pitch, but don't leave those who want to buy without an option either.

Make sure you also read Cliff Atkinson's awesome book, *Beyond Bullet Points*. It's one of the best on helping structure and create presentations that keep people interested and engaged.

Get to a podium

Every small business owner and marketer can benefit from becoming a better speaker. It doesn't really matter if your ambitions are to sell across the desk or present around the globe, getting your message heard and acted upon is essential.

In fact, I think that forcing yourself to get in front of an audience and deliver a talk of some sort is one of the best ways to develop competitive marketing skills. When you have to get your thoughts down into a concise thirty-minute talk, and then go out and get instant feedback from your audience, it develops character and poise along with an improved message.

The first time you get up in front of a crowd and realize that nobody will die if you aren't very polished, you might just get hooked on doing it again and again. In fact, when I was just getting started using speaking as a way to generate leads, I found that it was a tremendous referral source whether I was speaking to a room of hot prospects or a practice group. There always seemed to be someone in the audience who needed a speaker for another group they belonged to.

By using speaking that's based on education, you make it very easy to refer you and your business because you create very tangible evidence of your expertise by virtue of the fact that groups invite you to share your wisdom. Referring your business may be as easy as inviting a friend or colleague to come hear you present information on a current trend or pressing issue.

Bill Cates, author of *Unlimited Referrals*, gave me this tip: As you are just breaking into speaking, attend lots of events with speakers and make it a habit to seek out the speaker before the event and let them know what your business does and how it's unique. Make sure you tell them your name, sit near the front of the room during the presentation, and make sure your name tag is displayed prominently. I can tell you from experience on both ends of this scenario that you will probably get mentioned or called on by name by the speaker, creating a little attention and buzz for your business throughout the event.

Teaching business behavior

There is a well-worn truth that goes something like "If you want to learn something, teach it." I think this certainly applies to many aspects of business. If you want to learn something at a much deeper level, then write about it, speak about it, and create and conduct workshops and trainings on the subject. You can and should be doing all of these things as a routine part of your business growth.

However, I suggest that you take this concept to another level. I believe that there is a powerful layer to this teaching notion that is rarely accessed by small businesses. If you want your customers and partners to behave in certain ways, then teach them how to do it. Now, I'm not simply talking about teaching them how or what to buy—I mean teach them a behavior that clearly has a benefit to them, and ultimately benefits your cause as well.

- If you want to get more leads by getting up in front of groups and speaking, show your customers and partners how they might use this same strategy to generate leads for their own businesses. Hold workshops to teach them how to hold workshops.
- If you want to get more referrals from your strategic partners, conduct referral training sessions with your network and teach them how to build and activate a referral network.
- If you want to take advantage of a blog or other forms of social media, teach your staff, customers, and partners how to use online tools to build their businesses and get more of what they want.

It doesn't matter what business you're in. A manufacturer can benefit from this approach as much as a consultant. I can't overstate the power of this form of teaching. Beyond the fact that it will make you better at what you are teaching, it will help brand you and your business as an expert. It will help you build deeper relationships with your customers and partners, and it will definitely create a point of differentiation in your market.

Once you get a feel for this as a business strategy you can even begin to use it as a way to give back to your community. You can mentor fledgling businesses or show not-for-profits how to tap into your tactics.

Sources of content inspiration

I've talked a great deal about producing high-quality educational content as a way to get leads to know, like, and trust you.

At this point you're probably still wondering things like:

- How do know I what to write about?
- Where do I find good ideas?

▶ How do I uncover trends, tools, and tips that might appeal
to my audience?

The list below represents some of the places I turn to for content
inspiration. My favorite strategy is to mine these tools and sites for
seemingly unrelated ideas. I can't tell you how often I've uncovered the
seed of an idea from something totally unrelated to marketing that I
could twist to apply it in a totally new and relevant way.

Customer feedback—I love to turn customer and prospect questions into blog posts and more. You should be
keeping track of those FAQs and make your answer to
every single one available as content.

Delicious.com—This social bookmarking site is still my
favorite place to go and see what other folks are finding and saving.

Bing/xRank—Bing, the Microsoft search engine, seems to
turn up trends faster than Google Trends in its xRank
product.

Blogs—I use Google Reader, its RSS reader, to follow over
a hundred blogs regularly.

OneRiot—This is a real-time search engine that I use to
find the links that people on Twitter are discovering and
retweeting.

Keyword Phrases—Google's free keyword-search tools
can give you phrases that people are actually using to
find your products and services and offer some tips for
what to call your blog posts.

SmartBriefs—I subscribe to a daily briefing on a variety of
topics and see what some pretty smart editors are turning up.

***BusinessWeek*'s BX**—*BusinessWeek*'s social network allows
anyone to submit content on a large group of subjects.

Twitter—I follow some folks who are always finding and
tweeting good stuff. By setting a select group up in Tweet-
Deck I can always stay on top of these important tweets.

Magazines—I subscribe to *Wired, Inc., Entrepreneur, BusinessWeek*, and *Fast Company*, and while I sometimes get behind on the pile, I love to go there for inspiration.

Blend and repurpose

Throughout this chapter I've told you that educational content is king, and that's true. But now your head is swimming and you're thinking, "How do I create all this content when I've got a business to run? You say I need blogs, a newsletter, white papers, podcasts, training courses, instructional videos. . . . How do I get it all done?"

Yes, you do need all that stuff, and yes, it's a lot of work, so the trick is to find ways to take content you absolutely need to create and find ways to repurpose it. And to take content you've already produced and give it new life with new audiences.

- If you are doing an online demo, record it and put it on your Web site.
- If you get the same questions over and over again, answer them all in an audio format.
- Take those same questions and turn them into blog posts.
- Take several blog posts and stitch them together into an article to submit online and off.
- Create a series of seven related blog posts and you have a presentation.
- Write a white paper by posting questions to your blog and letting readers add their comments; turn the entire project into the white paper.
- Record all of your slide presentations and upload them to sites like YouTube and SlideShare.
- Schedule interviews with industry experts, and even with customers—record, transcribe, and publish them in several formats.
- Turn bits and bites of all of this into your monthly newsletter.

- Take something you've already written and break it down into bite-size chunks in multiple formats.
- Pitch your case studies to journalists as potential stories.

The key to making this way of content production a success is to always view your writing, speaking, selling, and research efforts with an eye on multiple uses. If you know you have to give a speech at a trade show next month, write it as blog content over the next five days and you've solved several needs at one time. Anything you produce should have several lives.

An important note: The word "repurpose" to me implies more than simply taking your newsletter and calling it a blog post. You've got to give it a bit of new life, new function, new delivery, new format, new spin. It's not that hard if you have that in mind as you create it.

Your content action plan

As we did in Chapter 5, now is a great time to pause and think through what we've covered in this chapter.

Your killer "technology"—What is the secret sauce or way of doing business that you plan to use to drive your content strategy?

Point-of-view white paper—What is the primary topic or outline for your point-of-view white paper?

Testimonial-gathering plan—How do you plan to gather testimonials from every happy customer?

What really triggers a referral—What customer phrases are important indicators of a need for what you offer?

Advertising for buzz—How can you utilize advertising to create awareness for your content?

PR for buzz—What is your plan for building relationships with key journalists to build awareness of your content?

Speaking for buzz—What topics, either trends or from your point-of-view white paper, would make great opportunities for you to get in front of audiences?

Teaching business behavior—What behavior or practice would you like to teach your customers and prospects to better understand?

Blend and repurpose—How many different ways can you use and reuse the content you create?

CHAPTER 7

Convergence Strategies

In Chapter 3 we introduced the idea of the highly converged business in this way: The highly converged business uses every advance in technology to open the opportunity for a deeper personal relationship. The highly converged business uses this principle as the primary filter for every marketing process, customer touch point, and tactic.

In this chapter you will find strategies and tactics you can employ to bring this high tech and high engagement together. Your convergence strategies are a natural extension of the content strategies covered in the previous chapter and lean very heavily on your commitment to creating content for maximum execution.

Take note that most effective conversion strategies also involve amplifying your customer's voice inside of your organization in highly wired and highly engaged ways.

Hub and spoke, online and off-line

Effective convergence relies on the creation of a primary hub of content, generally your company Web site, combined with spokes of content that open up pathways of awareness into every corner of your prospect's world—both online and off-line.

Your primary Web site is the place to house your company story, detailed descriptions of your products and services, customer success stories, shopping carts, contact details, white papers, FAQs, your blog, and any other video and audio content that helps a visitor discover more about why they might want to buy your products or engage your services. This site must be groomed and updated continuously to maintain maximum effectiveness, but it's not enough to take full advantage of what's possible through a total Web presence.

You should also consider some combination of:

- a Facebook page dedicated to changing content, events, videos, and announcements about every aspect of your business;
- a LinkedIn profile and frequent participation through the question and answer functionality;
- a Twitter account and a strategy to engage followers with updated content;
- active participation in business- or industry-specific social networking sites to create content awareness;
- a monthly e-mail newsletter with quick reads and deep dives into important subjects;
- an online Web conference series featuring industry-related guests or how-to information related to your industry (recorded, archived, and transcribed for even more content);
- audio and video success stories from real customers with proven and specific results;
- articles for submission to local, national, and industry-specific Web sites and publications;
- guest blog posts on high-profile or industry-specific blogs;
- a series of forty-five-minute seminars on trending and important topics that can be offered to strategic partners as a value add to their customers;
- custom RSS feeds that provide specific customers or prospects with filtered and aggregated information.

The changing face of being found

If lead generation has become about being found, the greatest enabler of this phenomenon has been the growing accuracy of (and corresponding consumer dependence upon) the search engine.

Smart marketers and widely referred businesses have taken full advantage of the market's addiction to finding information via search engines by creating the greatest possible number of opportunities for surfers to find their company's content when they go looking.

I'm talking about the very broad and sometimes abused business practice known as search engine optimization, but this activity has changed dramatically over the past few years. In the past, professionals and do-it-yourselfers spent half of their time optimizing every element on a page to get, or sometimes trick, the search engines to accept that a page was primarily about a handful of buried words or phrases. The other half of the SEO art lay in convincing other Web site owners and directories to link to their sites so search engines would assume that it must be valuable (or why would people be linking to it?). Both of these practices were abused.

Search engines and those using them have become more sophisticated. The shift has been from Web page optimization and link hounding to content and engagement optimization. In short, search engine optimization and the types of materials and activities common in social media are now undeniably intertwined. It has become extremely difficult to achieve any measure of success for important keyword phrases without the use of social media. (The flip side is that the organizations that take advantage of social media can dominate, particularly within industries slow to adapt.)

I'm not suggesting that Web page optimization and inbound links are no longer important; they are. They just aren't enough anymore. It is rare these days to do any kind of common search that does not return results from social media sites. Blog content dominates many question-related searches, and videos, audios, and images are routinely mixed into the search results.

What this means for the typical small business is that you must add a blog and podcast to the mix, upload images to Flickr, put customer testimonial videos on YouTube, write articles and press releases for EzineArticles and PitchEngine, create and brand profiles on Facebook, LinkedIn, Twitter, and industry-related social networking sites, and get very proactive about generating positive reviews on sites like Yelp!, Google Maps, and Insider Pages.

Any attempt to garner positive search results for your primary Web site hub must be accompanied by a strategy to optimize your entire Web presence through the effective use of social media.

The most easily referred companies are naturally social

One factor that isn't accurately measured in the world of social media is that companies that are very social are easier to refer. Companies that are very actively involved in social networking platforms and use many of the engagement tactics of traditional networking seem be the ones that just naturally generate more referrals.

Organizations that have historically relied on networking and face-to-face contact may naturally adopt the use of some of the more social aspects of high-tech engagement. It may be very easy for them to grasp the use of blog posts and comments; engage customers by inviting them to tell their stories in videos and audio recordings; engage partners by comarketing and packaging information; engage providers through collaboration practices and tools; and engage their staffs through shared brainstorming, wiki building, and storytelling.

In short, these firms are much easier to refer because they are simply making themselves easier to refer and be talked about—by using every social media tool available.

Networking redefined

One of the areas most intriguingly affected by the convergence within highly engaged and highly wired companies is networking. Many books written on the topic of referrals emphasize the practice of face-to-face networking as a key driver of referrals, and to a degree, I concur. However, like just about everything else in marketing, networking has changed dramatically as well.

The rise of social networking sites has introduced an entirely new set of tools. In a sense, traditional networking is closely tied to my concept of the highly engaged business while social networking is naturally aligned with the highly wired business. The trick then is to bring the best of both to each.

There was a time when you would meet a prospect or potential strategic partner at an industry function, exchange business cards, and possibly work toward scheduling an appointment to discover if there might be a relationship of some sort. If done authentically and patiently, this system often returns very positive results and is an essential business-building strategy.

Authentically and patiently means that each party approaches the possibility with a view not on selling but on discovering how they might benefit each other. The golden rule of "give to get" is on full display in effective networking.

But effective networking benefits greatly when content strategies are employed in conjunction with more traditional engagement. One of the hurdles in networking of any kind is building trust. When you have multiple sources of high-quality educational content you can send to a networking prospect, you build trust. When someone you meet at an industry breakfast can put your name in any search engine and find positive mentions and activity on page one, you build trust. When you invite a business owner you met at this month's Rotary meeting to share their story on your podcast, you get some great content, and you build trust.

Some emerging technology also allows you to personalize and automate your networking follow-up activity more easily. Let's say you meet Susan, the CEO of a start-up you've targeted, at a trade show mixer. You exchange business cards and then employ a service like enthusem (www.enthusem.com) to send Susan a personalized greeting card inviting her to download a free report or view a demo of the product you discussed. Once Susan visits the designated Web page, your salesperson receives an e-mail alert of it; knowing that Susan has taken a step indicating a level of interest suggests a follow-up is appropriate.

Other services, such as SendPepper (www.SendPepper.com), enable you to use automated e-mails and postcards featuring pURLs, or personalized URLs, to direct a message individually to each recipient. So instead of sending her to view your demo on a generic page, they are invited to it at susan.productdemo.com. Of course, when she does, you receive an alert.

The key is to view these technologies in tandem with your face-to-face, authentic networking activities and not as an either-or proposition. The key to standing out is to do both engagement and wired better than anyone else.

Some networking power tools

As I stated above, networking at events attended by your ideal customers is still a great way to make some nice introductions and start gently spreading the word about your products and services. There is a bit of art to this and plenty of bad examples evoking the worst used-car stereotypes imaginable.

Keep these simple rules in mind and you will be fine:

1. Think "what am I here to give?"
2. Speak only to educate; don't try to sell anything

Scott Ginsberg, whose story I shared in Chapter 1, has some great tools on his Web site for making the art of relationship building a little more fun, particularly for those who aren't naturally comfortable with it.

His free e-book, *Let Me Ask Ya This . . .* : 55 *Questions to Ask Someone You Just Met* (www.hellomynameisscott.com/lmayt.pdf), is a real winner, and quite frankly also includes some gems to ask people you already know—your existing clients.

Another tool Scott uses is something he calls My Card. This is a blank card with lines on it. When he meets someone who has forgotten to carry their business card, he whips out a blank My Card and records their information, then he gives them some to use as well.

Social networking

Social networking sites such as Facebook have grown in popularity in part because for some networking online is a lot easier—or so it seems. Many people mistake the surface engagement you can create on Twitter or LinkedIn for complete networking.

Authentic networking is authentic networking no matter what the platform. One of the greatest benefits of participating on social networking sites is the ability to easily gain access to millions of otherwise hard-to-reach targeted prospects. But, that's the danger as well.

Social networking sites have become very successful because they've done a great job building the wired tools that make it very easy for people to find each other, engage in conversations, and keep in communication. But, to make these sites the most effective for your business-building and referral efforts, you must use the engagement tactics of traditional networking. I like to use the cocktail party analogy. If you went to a cocktail party, you wouldn't walk up to the first person you saw and start talking about yourself or, worse, pitching your insurance products. Would you? But that's what so many people do when it comes to social networking online.

Using social networking sites effectively begins with finding ways to discover potential relationships easily. In my opinion this is done following a multipronged approach:

1. Publish content and links to things such as your blog posts and webinars on sites such as Facebook and Twitter, so that participants in these networks can find you by way of your content.
2. Amplify other people's content on social networks and in your own blog posts as a way to build relationships.
3. Make a habit of sharing great content from trusted sources you discover from your own research through your RSS reader and other social bookmarking sites such as Delicious or Digg.
4. Ask and answer questions on LinkedIn, Twitter, and

Facebook as a way of engaging prospects and getting feedback.

5. Be authentic and human when you participate and let your educational content hub do all the selling.

The original social networks

Much is made of the fabulous growth of online social networks such as MySpace and LinkedIn.

But let's not forget the opportunities available in the original social networks—schools, community organizations, and religious institutions. In every community in America, thousands of word-of-mouth referrals are made while attending a kindergarten graduation, a sporting event, or a Sunday social.

Widely referred businesses still look for opportunities to tap into this natural marketing phenomenon. The trick is to partner, offer value, and forget trying to exploit relationships in the network. There are few businesses that can't approach these community-based groups and propose a win-win promotion. Most have multiple fundraising needs as a whole as well as within subgroups such as PTAs, Scout troops, and soup kitchens. Product and professional service providers alike should consider these community-based partners.

Lead nurturing is personal

Once you discover that your converged networking activity produces the fruit of a lead, you can further employ an engaged and wired approach to move your lead along the path of know, like, and trust by providing them the precise information they require, at the precise time they require it.

Marketers have long concluded that most leads, even those referred by a friend, need time and contact to develop trust. One of the ways this is accomplished is through a planned set of contacts delivered over time. From an engaged point of view, this can be accomplished through a series of letters, phone calls, invitations, and briefings. By employing the latest technology, a converged approach emerges that makes the engagement much more informed and effective. Integrating your lead nurturing into customer relationship management (CRM) software such as ACT!, you can create drip marketing campaigns that deliver to your planned contacts based on actions taken by your lead.

Let's say you receive ten referred leads. You can set up campaigns that send a postcard to all ten inviting them to click on a link for more information. The five who click get an automatic e-mail message inviting them to attend a webinar next week, while the five who did not click receive an e-mail offering a free downloadable tips sheet. The five webinar invitees are immediately funneled to the sales team for a phone contact.

Again, the overriding theory of convergence is that engagement and technology are employed hand in hand to create efficiency married with the ability to deliver deeper engagement, not as a shield against personal engagement.

But what's a highly wired business to do to create more engagement?

Much of this discussion surrounding convergence has centered on finding ways to tap new technologies and platforms to create deeper engagement. Some firms, however, are wired at their core, and are naturally drawn to high-tech marketing solutions, but need a little help creating convergence using more traditional engagement tactics.

If you find yourself in that camp, here are a few idea starters to help you create more personal engagement with customers:

- Call five a day and thank them. Go through your customer list and randomly call five per day and thank them for their business. Get in the habit of calling customers and asking what more you could do. Send handwritten notes. Apologize for ignoring them if you have been!
- Segment your customers. Not all customers are created equal, so treat them individually. Your most profitable,

referring customers should get VIP treatment. You don't have to downgrade anyone, just make sure your best customers know who they are.

- Bring them together. Often your customers are peers and might enjoy the opportunity to commiserate with a group of peers, or at least network, over lunch.

- Create a marketing board. Your best customers are probably advocates for your business, whether you know it or not. Create an informal board of your most involved customers and ask for their input and accountability in the development of your marketing strategies and tactics, even if you have to meet via Web conference.

Get out from behind the computer and go out there in your customer's world and get a better understanding of what they are going through, and you may just discover an entirely new view of your customers and how you can engage them more fully.

Blog as convergence generator

I happen to believe that a blog offers one of the best routes to accomplishing much of what we are covering in this chapter, and it's no surprise that widely referred businesses have very active blogs. Now, for many a blog still seems like a trendy tool used mostly by online businesses, but nothing could be further from the truth. Remember how often I've talked about producing lots of educational content that helps your prospects find your business when they go looking for solutions? A blog is by far the easiest way to create content that ranks well in the search engines. So don't think of a blog as a publication or journal that people are going to sit down and read on a daily basis. Think of it as a management system for your content that's automatically search engine friendly.

In Chapter 4 I introduced the 4 Cs—content, context, connection, and community. A well-written-and-maintained blog has the ability to deliver all four of these elements. That's why I often refer to a blog as the front door to the entire convergence strategy concept. In fact, I've rarely encountered a business that cannot use a blog as the catalyst for all forms of online engagement.

Hidden benefits of blogging

I've personally written a blog for quite some time now, and I can state without hesitation that it's the single greatest business asset I own. It's led to countless interviews with national publications, my first book deal, and interactions with hundreds of thousands of small-business owners. My blog is an incredible source of search engine traffic and exposure for my products and services. But even if none of that were true, knowing what I know now, I would still write a blog.

Some of the most profound benefits of the blog-writing practice are available to anyone, with or without any substantial following. It's not that we call it a new media marketing term like blog or that the software used by bloggers possesses some magical power, it's that the act of writing something, something about my business and passion, something that I observe that touches me, something I learn and can't wait to share, is intrinsically rewarding. I did not start blogging for these other reasons, but they are the reasons I continue to advocate blogging for everyone:

> **Blogging makes me a better thinker**—In an effort to create content for a blog that is succinct, reveals new ways to look at everyday things, or applies simple solutions to seemingly complex problems, I believe I now think about business much differently.
>
> **Blogging makes me a better listener**—When I engage in conversations or listen to radio interviews, I listen with a writer's ear, and I often find my head filling up with blog post ideas simply by listening to others discuss sometimes unrelated subjects.
>
> **Blogging makes me a better writer**—The fact that I practice writing daily has made me a better writer. It doesn't mean I'm the world's greatest writer, but doing

something makes you better at it—it's hard to deny that. Of course, writing publicly like this also allows for community reaction to help you get better faster.

Blogging makes me a better salesperson—I write like I speak, and often I write to sell an idea or even a very specific tactic. It's amazing, but I find that clearly stating idea pitches in writing has improved my ability to articulate them quickly in a selling or interview setting. It's like you build up this reserve bank of preprogrammed discussion points.

Blogging makes me a better speaker—This one leads nicely from the previous point, but I'll also add that working through blog posts on meatier topics, those that readers can't help but weigh in on, has produced some of my best presentation material to date.

Blogging keeps me focused on learning—The discipline required to create even somewhat interesting content in the manner I've chosen requires that I study lots of what's hot, what's new, what's being said, and what's not being said in order to find ways to apply it to the world of small business.

Blogging allows me to test out ideas—I've made some incredible discoveries about some of my ideas—and yes, had a few flops, too—based on the immediate and sometimes passionate responses from readers.

Blogging makes me a better networker—I have developed hundreds of relationships with other writers that provide me with ideas, tips, and resources to share and who willingly pass on mine. Some of these relationships remain professional, but some have evolved into very fulfilling personal relationships as well. (Sharing a beer at a conference helps that along.)

Blogging allows me to create bigger ideas—This one is related to testing out ideas, but the habit of producing content over time also affords you the opportunity to create larger editorial ideas that can be reshaped and repurposed for other settings. I've taken a collection of blog posts on a specific topic and turned them into an e-book more than once.

My hope is that, if you're one of those business folks who has been blogging but doesn't know if it's worth it, or you've held off because you don't think anyone wants to read a blog written by you, this list of added benefits will give you the leverage of long-term experience sufficient to help you keep at it or get started.

Creating a blog

Blogging software such as WordPress (WordPress.org) has evolved to the point where most businesses can build their entire site on this software originally conceived as a blogging only tool. As previously stated, blogging software is the easiest way to create content that is search-engine friendly. This attribute goes for creating traditional static Web pages as well. Once your blogging software is set up, you, or anyone you assign, can create what appear to be traditional static HTML Web pages as well, such as a home page, product pages, contact pages, and other core Web pages as easily as creating a new blog post.

While installing blog software may seem like a daunting task for some, it's not terribly difficult, and there are many free resources full of tips and tutorials. One of my favorites is a site called Yoast (www .yoast.com). The more visual learner might also enjoy the video tutorials at WordPress.tv. If you want to get more from your WordPress blog and interact with an active community of their users, you might check out WordPress Tavern (www.wptavern.com). These sites go far beyond the basic installation and setup lessons. You can find a great deal of information about blogging and attracting readership in general.

The template system utilized by most blogging software allows you to add and edit pages from a very user-friendly dashboard, enabling anyone in your organization to make frequent changes and additions without the aid of a Web programmer. WordPress designers have created thousands of free and premium templates that make it very simple and affordable to create entire Web sites built on their engine. This approach makes it very easy to then make the blogging component of your site a premier feature.

Harsh blogging reality: No one is reading your blog

Lest you think I view blogging as the marketing magic bullet, I feel the need to share some harsh words lifted from one of my favorite bloggers and blog, Sonia Simone senior editor for Copyblogger (www .copyblogger.com):

> As far as anyone can figure, there are about 200 million blogs around the world. Technorati tells us there are about 900,000 blog posts made every 24 hours.
>
> The world is not waiting breathlessly to hear what you have to say about losing weight with acai berries, making big money as an affiliate marketer, or how to join your Secrets of the Breakthrough Millionaire Insider Guru Mastermind Platinum Club.
>
> Me-too content gets ignored. Scraped and remixed junk won't cut it. There's too much good content that you need to compete with. And there's no magic system that can replace sitting in front of your keyboard and producing something that somebody wants to read. (Or partnering with someone who can.)
>
> If you don't have a great answer to the question, "Why should anyone read your blog?" you're going to be pretty unhappy with your results. That's why we spend so much time teaching you how to produce better, smarter, more effective content.

Blogging best practices

Simply uploading blog software to your server, posting once or twice, and calling it a blog is not going to cut it. I've given the discussion of a blog for your business a lot of space in this chapter for good reason: It's an essential marketing element. You don't maximize essential marketing elements with little or no effort. Effectively taking advantage of all that a blog has to offer your business requires that you invest serious input.

There are a few things that you must do before you ever start blogging or attempting to reactivate your long-dormant blog project.

1. Use a tool such as Google Reader (google.com/reader) to subscribe to industry-related blogs, your competitor's blogs (many have them!), and other popular blogs. Reading these blogs can teach you how bloggers write, what they typically write about, and how they interact with readers and other bloggers. This doesn't mean you will simply copy what your competitors do, but it can help inform your overall blogging strategy.

2. Blogging software has a built-in functionality that allows readers to add comments to posts. This ability to interact is one of the reasons blogs have become so popular. Add relevant comments to a handful of the blogs you subscribed to in step one above. Participating in this manner gives you another view of how bloggers interact with readers and is a practice that can open up pathways back to your Web site as other readers view your comments and decide you have something valuable to say.

3. Now that you are reading relevant blogs and participating on them through comments, you're ready to create your own. There are many books and services that can help you with the technical details of creating a blog, but my primary advice here is that you look at the WordPress.org software that installs on your Web-hosting server.

Post often

Over the past few years I can easily say that the number one question I get asked about blogging is "How often do I need to write a post?" Unfortunately, what these people are really asking is "How do I get the benefits of a blog without actually writing anything?" And the answer, of course, is that you can't, but that doesn't mean you have to feel compelled to blog three or four times a day, even if you see some people doing this.

Your blog content strategy should be based on your overall marketing strategy. For most that means the blog is not a source of advertising revenues when page views matter above all else. Rather, it's a content creation and search engine optimization tool. With that in mind, you do need to commit to creating new content a minimum of three to four times a week to get the greatest long-term benefits.

Keyword rich

When it comes to making a determination about what to actually write on your blog, search engine benefits need to be high on the list of considerations. You should focus many of your posts on the actual words and phrases that your ideal customers use when searching for a business or product like yours. Using actual search phases, including local terms, in the title of your posts is a good way to have your posts show up high on the list when prospects conduct searches using them. Tools such as Wordtracker (freekeywords.wordtracker.com), SEO Book (tools.seobook.com), and Google Search–based Keyword Tool (www.google.com/sktool) can help you better understand the actual phrases people use when they turn to search engines looking for answers.

You do want to focus on creating content that is interesting and relevant to your prospects, and often this is simply a matter of collecting and answering, in the form of blog posts, the real questions that prospects pose in the sales process, and perhaps a few they should be posing but don't consider. This can be a nice way to create some additional convergence on your blog. Consider polling your customers to find out what they would like you to write about, what questions they have, what they love about your products or services and would like you to amplify. Getting your customers to participate, either by way of content suggestions or comments, will make your blog more useful, and probably more rewarding for you and your staff to write.

Create engagement

After you start blogging, you need to become an active participant in reader engagement. This goes beyond some of the natural marketing things you might do to let people know your blog address, such as announcing it in your marketing materials and placing the URL on business cards and e-mail signatures. Active engagement starts by inviting readers to participate, in this case through the comment function.

The follow seven tactics will help you get more comments and more engagement.

> **Ask for comments**—Sometimes just creating a post and inviting your readers to add comments is all it takes to get them flowing. But usually commenting is a habit that you need to build up in your readership over time.
>
> **Ask questions and seek opinions**—From time to time ask your readers what they think of something, or what they have done that works, or how they have addressed a particularly challenging situation. You don't need to have all the answers.
>
> **Comment on comments**—When readers comment you can encourage additional conversation by responding and showing that comments are welcome—even if the comment calls something you said into question.
>
> **Show some humanity**—No matter what your topic, readers like to know that the author is a human being. It's okay to let that show and to add personal thoughts. Only you can determine how far to go with this, but readers will connect more once they know your story.
>
> **Stir the pot from time to time**—You don't have to be a celebrity gossip blogger to stir up a little controversy. Often some of my best interactions come from topics that people are decidedly passionate about.
>
> **Make comment participation a game**—Keep score and reward your most active commentators. There is a WordPress plugin called Top Commentators that keeps track of how many comments a particular reader makes and rewards them with a link. Plugins are generally free tools that can be added to almost any online Web site or application to give it more functionality. You can find hundreds of them in the WordPress Directory (word press.org/extend/plugins).

Make sure commenting is easy—Publish your comment feed and consider adding a Subscribe to Comments plugin so that people get an e-mail notice when someone responds to a post they have commented on. This practice has the impact of bringing back those who make comments to view the additions. This is one of the best ways to turn your comments into conversations.

Multiple blog authors

Once you get your blog up and running and develop a natural rhythm for creating and posting content, consider inviting other authors. Perhaps you have multiple authors already, or use various folks in your marketing department to post content, but I'd like to suggest another approach.

Dell Computer wanted to focus on building a community that acknowledged what they saw as a new kind of worker they referred to as the "digital nomad." To them, there were growing numbers of people taking work with them, connecting wherever they were, and working wherever they could get an Internet connection. These folks were also great targets for many of the company's products, but rather than broadcast sales messages to them about Dell's suite of tools, they created a community called Digital Nomads (www.digitalnomads.com) where they could come and find content produced by a select group of trusted bloggers, who wrote about everything from the best airport to get sushi at to what laptop bags and jackets were the best for air travel.

The multiblogger community quickly become a favorite haunt for people living or wanting to live the digital lifestyle. Community members were also encouraged to tell their travel-, work-, and tool-related tips and stories.

Podcast and become a journalist

The hype over this thing called podcasting peaked long ago. So much so that you either don't hear much about it anymore in the media, or you hear that it's "so last year." While it's true that the bloom is off the rose, podcasting's usefulness as a marketing tool for the small business is better than ever.

Let me break down what podcasting is from a marketing point of view. It's the use of simple tools to create multimedia content, engage prospects and customers alike, and open doors to strategic partners like never before. If any of those things sound like useful objectives, then podcasting is for you. (Not to mention the possibilities for using this approach to create products.)

Here's how I would suggest you think about podcasting as a convergence tool:

A great way to feature the stories of your best customers—Interview your customers and post their stories for prospects to hear. It doesn't matter if you have a large audience for your podcast; your customers will dig the attention and you'll get content on the fly.

A great way to open doors—When you contact an author, industry leader, or expert of any kind with the offer to interview and feature them on your podcast, you'll be amazed at the quality of guest you can secure and the exposure that can bring. If you run a print shop in the middle of Des Moines, you can offer your customers and prospects access to the leading design, print, and color experts from around the world—wouldn't that be valuable?

A great way to build and solidify your strategic network—By routinely interviewing the members of your network of partners, you can strengthen that network and make referrals to them more easily.

A great competitive advantage—Does your competitor have an interview with the current president of your trade association on their site? You can combine two of these ideas by holding live Web conferences using either interviews or presentations, record the live presentation, and voilà, you've also created your next podcast episode.

Can you see how these advantages might make podcasting a killer small-business tool?

The good news is that you don't have to invest in all kind of studio equipment to produce a quality interview series. You need several elements connected together to start creating your podcast. I'll list each item and give some suggestions for tools and services to explore.

Record—To record you will need a decent microphone and computer recording software. If you are doing phone interviews (I recommend it for ease and convenience), then you can use SkypeIn, a free service that provides you with a phone number for your guest to call. I also use a low-cost Skype (skype.com) add-on called Call Recorder so I can record the call directly to my computer. I use a Blue Snowball USB microphone and Bose headphones.

Edit—You may want to edit your interviews for length, or to add music and sound effects. GarageBand (www.apple .com/support/garageband/edit), a program that comes on Macs, is very adequate for this, and many PC users like a free program called Audacity (audacity.sourceforge .net). Both programs also compress audio recordings into the preferred mp3 format.

Host—Even compressed mp3 recordings can be rather larger, so it's a good idea to use a media-hosting service. This may not be an issue if you don't receive many listens and downloads, but I like to use a service called Libsyn (www.libsyn.com), because it's very inexpensive and streams thousands of plays effortlessly.

Promote—You'll want to let the world know about your interviews, and one of the easiest ways is to use blogging software such as WordPress to describe each show and provide a link to the recording (you can see how I host the *Duct Tape Marketing* podcast at www .ducttapemarketing.com/blog/category/podcast/) A further advantage to using blogging software is that it automatically produces an RSS feed that can be read and retrieved by podcast directories and, most important, iTunes. (this way people can get your shows on their iPods and iPhones.)

Once you get your recording and posting system set up, you will find a tremendous return on the investment in the podcast if you think guest access first and listenership second. You can take this as far as you like, but just adding basic audio interviews to your site is an easy way to take your content to the next level.

Audio as a customer service tool

Web marketers have known the value of adding audio to Web sites and sales pages for a number of years now. Used properly, audio can really help visitors connect, get directions, and become more excited about a product or service (video is quickly jumping into this space too).

One overlooked use of audio is to help enhance your customer's experience with you, your products, and your services. Adding audio messages throughout your Web site can guide your visitor's experience in many ways.

For example you can add:

- Audio welcome messages on thank-you pages or in automatically generated e-mail
- How-to audio links delivered with products: When someone places an order online or off, you can send a link to an audio recording that gives them helpful instructions.
- Personalized instructions to help listeners get more from a service—imagine sending a new customer orientation message with a greeting from their customer service rep.

- Getting-started audios to help a client know what to do next
- Send an audio greeting that recaps your just completed message and details agreed-upon next steps. (A free service called Jott allows you to record a voice memo through your phone and have them transcribed and sent via e-mail.)
- Conference call summaries for nonattendees; record quick audio recaps of the important details of a call
- Assignments for third-party vendors or collaborators: Post audio messages and instructions.
- A FAQ page with the questions posed via audio from real prospects and clients and your expert answers or those of real clients spoken for each. Customers or prospects could be given a call-in number to ask their questions, and then you could answer them via audio as well.

I use a very effective service for these types of audio enhancements called Audio Acrobat (www.audioacrobat.com). I like it most for its ease of use. The service allows you to record or upload audio files from your computer microphone or telephone and then turns them into a streaming mp3 and creates a nifty little audio player that you can easily paste anywhere on your Web site, and even send through e-mail. You can also create guest lines and allow clients to record audio messages, such as testimonials, via telephone, and then turn those into Web content as well. The guest-line feature operates very much like voice mail. People call a special number you've given them, leave a message, and then you grab a little code to place their audio message and player on your site. I've also seen podcasters use this guest feature to take recorded audience calls and drop them into shows.

Make video an everyday marketing activity

Capturing and adding video to your marketing and social media mix has become a necessary and increasingly expected part of creating overall marketing messages. The ability to create engaging content that amplifies your customer's voice in the marketing process is a key convergence approach.

With each passing day this task just seems to get easier. Camera prices have fallen while quality has risen; editing software is free and simple to use; and video hosting and streaming from sites like YouTube provide most of the heavy lifting when it comes to putting those videos online.

Pocket-size HD video cameras have created the opportunity for every marketer and every salesperson to create engaging video content on the fly.

Here is a handful of ways to think about capturing and creating video content:

- Have each salesperson gather customer success stories and testimonials during sales calls
- Record customers giving your product a test or demonstration
- Capture usability testing as you record people interacting with your Web site
- Record short videos of your strategic partners talking about their relationship with your firm
- Capture highlights from every booth you visit at a trade show
- Record salespeople giving successful sales presentations
- Tour your office and record a "meet our staff member" video each week

And, my two personal favorites from a convergence standpoint:

- Hold a contest and ask your customers to submit videos of themselves using your product, or even just interacting with your brand in some fashion
- Offer to pay your customers for submitting training or tips videos showing people how to use or get more out of your products

The use of video will only grow more and more important, so making it easy to capture video moments is one of the keys to getting in the habit of playing this game. To get the greatest impact for your videos from a search engine standpoint, you'll want to take the time to optimize them on hosting sites such as YouTube.

Don't just upload the videos and move on, take time to create:

> **Title**—YouTube allows you to name your video. Make sure to choose a keyword-rich title that clearly cues what the video is about: How to Hire an Attorney.
>
> **Description**—This is where you get to describe, perhaps in a hundred words or so, exactly what's in the video. (Search engines don't watch your video, so this is partly how they decide what it's a about.) This should also include several variations of keywords searchers might use.
>
> **Tags**—These are one- and two-word phrases that help the search engines categorize your video—marketing, plumbing, social media. You can use many of these, so add as many as you can think of, and be sure to include variations—how to and howto, for instance.

I've focused primarily on YouTube here, but there are other video-hosting sites, such as Viddler and Vimeo (www.vimeo.com) worth looking into as well. You might also consider learning about a service called tubemogul (www.tubemogul.com) that allows you to upload your video one time and have it distributed to many video-hosting sites, increasing your exposure to the users of many video sites.

For more tips and tutorials on the use of video in marketing, visit ReelSEO (www.reelseo.com)—a great online video marketing resource.

Let's do eLunch

As more and more people work virtually, acquire clients globally, and scramble to get it all done in a day, the concept of "meeting" has changed. Of course, much of this change is due to technology that enables us to interact in somewhat human ways while around the world or, for that matter, around the community. So-called eLunches are a new and highly efficient way to meet people (while saving a little piece of the planet, too). I think the idea of doing lunch virtually adds a little more creative differentiation to your pitch.

The idea behind an eLunch is much like a lunch meeting you might do at the local deli, but both parties meet while sitting at their desks. In order to pull this off in a way that gives it some authenticity, you can use a Web video meeting technology (yes, you've got to get out of your pajamas and smile for the camera) such as Skype video chat, Dimdim (www.dimdim.com), or iLinc Video Conferencing (www.ilinc .com). You'll also need food.

Because your guest might be anywhere in the world, a safe bet is to set up an account with a national chain such as Pizza Hut and send a pizza to your guest to enjoy during your eLunch. This might be a good way to get a meeting with you to stand out a bit.

Now, I understand a chain-store pizza might not be your idea of way to impress a potential client, so if you want to take this up a notch you can go for a more upscale chain that delivers, or if you want to really score points, see if your meeting prospect has a Twitter account, blog, or other social profile your can access and scan for mentions of local favorites or vegetarian leanings. Imagine how impressed your prospect will be when that shitake mushroom sandwich from their local vegan hangout shows up for your lunch.

Everyone needs an angle to get to the table, and an eLunch just might be yours.

Solve problems publicly

Over the course of the few years a great deal of customer service has moved online to social networking platforms like Twitter. Just about any company that offers online products and services should be providing tech support to Twitter requests. The expectation is growing that companies provide a level of support for some users using this platform.

I often turn to Twitter first to engage support for the tools I use. From a convergence standpoint, this approach offers the ability to solve customer support issues and answer information requests in a public forum. While this may scare some, I think it offers the opportunity to demonstrate your service practices in full view of potential customers, providing a level of proof of what you promise. If your company is considering exploring Twitter for support, here are a couple ideas and a handful of tools that might make the task of providing service from your company a little easier than sitting 24/7 at your laptop.

Create a company support account and give it a company-branded avatar. (An avatar is the small image or photo associated with your name or account.) Some large organizations have numerous folks participating on Twitter and choose to use a personal name combined with some sort of company branding. For example, one Hewlett-Packard social media profile is AngelaAtHP.

Remember, this is support, pure and simple, so folks aren't really looking to engage with @Chuckie. It's OK for several folks in an organization to monitor and respond under one branded avatar. It's also OK for support to come from a real social media person, but you may find yourself rotating people through this position as well.

The next step is "search routines." You need to set up searches at search.twitter.com for your brands, products, and company and monitor them using a tool like TweetDeck or Splitweet so that you can know when someone is asking about, complaining about, or praising what you're tracking so you can respond.

Listening in a digital age

Listening to the wants and needs of your markets and customers has always been a good idea. Any good salesperson can tell you the benefits of listening—if you do it right the prospect will always reveal how to get the sale.

In today's rapidly shifting business environment listening is one of the key competitive tactics, but the sheer volume of what's being said makes it a more complicated exercise. The days of spending a little time down at the barbershop to measure the pulse of the market are long past.

One of the ways that you can more fully participate in the content and convergence strategies we've been exploring is to also employ a powerful set of digital ears to monitor and engage in the millions of conversations going on simultaneously in every corner of town and every corner of the planet. By setting up filtering, aggregating, and alert technology or services you can gain access to real-time conversations about the following:

- Your customer's ongoing experience
- Any brand/product/CEO mentions
- Complaints about competing services
- Inaccurate information about your organization
- The thoughts and needs of journalists in your industry

The key is to create, either on your own or through paid services, a dashboard that delivers the conversations surrounding topics of interest right to your inbox or browser as part of your measurement suite of analytics.

Your do-it-yourself toolbox should include:

Google Alerts (www.google.com/alerts)—This tool allows you to set up searches for any phrase and receive e-mail or RSS alerts any time that phrase shows up online.

Search.twitter.com—Monitoring Twitter can be seen as a separate stream (Google has added Twitter and other social media conversations to results, and eventually search results that include conversations happening about a subject in real-time will be the norm for all search engines.) Using the advanced search function allows you to set up very specific searches, even including geographic details. These searches produce RSS feeds that you can then subscribe to.

tweetbeep.com—Similar to Google Alerts but for Twitter. You simply create the search phrases you want to track, and you receive notification any time your phrases show up in Twitter conversations.

BoardTracker.com—Focuses on the most popular bulletin-board conversations and can turn up responses that don't show up anywhere else. Some industries still have very heavy bulletin-board use.

BackType.com—This is a search tool that focuses on blog comments. Blog comments don't often make it into the mainstream search results, so this is a way to listen in on this set of content.

Social Mention (www.socialmention.com)—This is a mash-up search engine of many of the formats of content, such as audio and video. I've found it to be a nice way to turn up mentions that don't occur anywhere else.

Many organizations may find that the ability to listen in digitally is so important or so time-consuming that they need to employ a paid service to do it. These services also offer countless ways to filter and analyze the data you collect, far more than you might be able to on your own. The greater level of analysis is a great way to spot trends, find opportunities, and measure ROI for your online marketing efforts.

Some popular paid services include:

- Radian6 (www.radian6.com)—robust set of analytics, relates data in some very cool ways
- Trackur (www.trackur.com)—advanced set of tools, well worth the cost
- BuzzLogic (www.buzzlogic.com)—focuses on helping you find key influencers driving conversations.
- Filtrbox (www.filtrbox.com)—very easy to use, powerful and low cost

While paid tracking services do indeed involve costs, the amount of information that can be tracked and, perhaps more important, analyzed in sophisticated ways may make it well worth the expense. Services such as the ones above can filter comments related to trends, tone, and consistent points of view in ways that can help companies uncover competitors' weaknesses and spot opportunities for new products and services.

A social media system example

Throughout this chapter I've referred to social media participation on numerous occasions as an enabler of conversion strategies. For many businesses, even those that recognize the benefit of this approach, the chore is in figuring out how to manage what seems like a daunting task of yet more to do.

For me personally the trick was to develop and employ a systematic approach to social media participation that takes into consideration my overall marketing strategies, desired level of engagement, and sanity. Here's an overview of how I do that. (Understand that the quickly evolving nature of this topic means that by the time you read this much will have changed, but this gives you an idea of a routine.)

Twice daily

- Check Twitter via TweetDeck—preset searches for @ducttape, john jantsch, and duct tape marketing. Respond as I see fit; follow some @replies that seem appropriate.
- Scan mybloglog. I obsess over traffic, but this reveals trending links and stumble surges in real time so I can react if appropriate.
- Respond to comments on my blog

Once daily

- Write a blog post. RSS subs get it, Twitter tools send to Twitter; Facebook gets it, FriendFeed updates
- Scan Twitter followers for relevant conversations to join

- Scan Google Reader subscriptions to read and stimulate ideas
- Share Google Reader favs. Publish these to Facebook and FriendFeed
- Fleck Tweet (fleck.com/lite) any blog pages from my subscriptions that I love—this goes to Twitter
- Bookmark any blog pages from my subscriptions that I love: Delicious using Firefox plugin for right-click posting. This goes to FriendFeed.
- StumbleUpon (www.stumbleupon.com) blog pages from my subscriptions that I love. This goes to Facebook and FriendFeed.
- Scan Google Alerts for my mentions of name, brand, and products—in Google Reader as RSS feed. Respond as appropriate.
- Add comments to blogs as appropriate—mostly response types—using Google Reader and BackType

Weekly (End of Week)
- Scan LinkedIn Questions from my network and respond when appropriate
- Scan Delicious, Digg, and mixx popular (www.mixx.com/popular) and select bookmarks for content ideas and trending topics
- Consciously add comments to conversations I want to join—hot-topic focused
- Join one Twitter hot trend conversation if appropriate; search.Twitter.com shows these in real time

Monthly
- Check Mr. Tweet (mrtweet.com), a tool that recommends people to follow based on common interests
- Scan Amazon's upcoming and new releases for authors to interview on podcast (the big names seem more accessible with a book release coming!)
- Post a press release with social media links to online

press release distribution services PitchEngine or PRWeb (prweb.com). This changes depending on what's going on, but post at least monthly.

▶ Strategize on ways to repurpose and repackage any and all of this in ways that make it more accessible to another audience.

For some this just seems crazy—others will notice some obvious glaring holes in this system. The point, though, is the system approach. Set up your system and work it, day in and day out, whatever that means for you, and then you will start to understand the vital role that social media can come to play in your overall marketing strategy.

Your convergence action plan

Wow, lots of information overload again. My hope is that while you've come to this point in our journey thinking big picture and strategically, you've also started to implement and act on some items you've discovered. But, once again, let's pause and scratch out an action plan for this important topic of convergence.

Hub and spoke, online and off-line—If your primary Web site is your content hub, where will you create spokes to your ideal clients?

The changing face of being found—What is your plan to optimize your content, including audio, video and profiles?

Networking redefined—How will you merge the authentic aspects of traditional networking with the opportunities that exist in social networking?

Lead nurturing is personal—What technologies, campaigns, and personal touches can you bring to the process of moving a lead from know, like, and trust to try and buy?

Blog as convergence generator—What is your plan to create and optimize a blogging tool as your primary content and convergence generator?

Multiple blog authors—How and when can you get customers, partners, and staff also creating content on behalf of your convergence strategy?

Podcast and become a journalist—Who could you interview and record as a content and convergence tool?

Audio as a customer service tool—How can you employ technology to get your customers involved in creating content and providing customer service?

Make video an everyday marketing activity—How will you take advantage of the growing effectiveness and expectation of video content?

Solve problems publicly—How can you move customer service and sales questions out into the public view?

Listening in a digital age—What items belong on a dashboard that allows you to monitor all that is being said about your brand?

A social media system example—What social media activities could you create routines around?

CHAPTER 8

Your Customer Network

The quickest route to a healthy business and serious referral momentum is a customer, or what I also like to call a "direct network member," who is beyond satisfied and willing to voluntarily tell the world all
about your business. But it's not enough to simply provide a good product or service; that's probably the minimum of what is expected. Your
marketing, sales, content, and service must all converge in a systematic
fashion to move your customers through the lifecycle we outlined in
Chapter 4—know, like, trust, try, buy, repeat, and refer.

In this chapter we are going to discuss creating a systematic referral approach that involves identifying your customer champions, educating and equipping them, developing processes to build referrals into
your selling process, measuring and communicating results, and building a culture and community of referrals as part of your overall customer platform.

What's your referral number?

I can tell you that the relative health and success of most businesses
can be gauged by this simple factor—how many clients refer friends,
neighbors, and colleagues.

This may be hard for some to hear, but if you are not receiving lots of referrals, there is something that needs fixing. So what's your referral number? What percentage of your clients refer business? If you can track that number, you've got a great starting place to build from. Installing processes that allow you to capture the source of every lead, such as surveying or asking prospects how they heard of you, using tracking codes in direct mail or on Web pages, and creating custom fields in your prospect contact database or CRM software to note referral sources are a couple of simple tracking steps. Understanding the baseline of that one metric is key to fixing it through many of the strategies and tactics we've discussed so far.

In Fred Reichheld's book *The Ultimate Question* he introduced something called the Net Promoter Score (NPS). NPS is based on the fundamental perspective that every company's customers can be divided into three categories: promoters, passives, and detractors. By asking one simple question—How likely is it that you would recommend us to a friend or colleague?—you can track these groups and get a clear measure of your company's performance through the customer's eyes.

In a way, everything we've discussed in this book to this point has led to this question. That's because it's not just a matter of fixing or improving your products and services. That's important, but equally important is attracting and working with the right customers. Most of the folks that NPS would categorize as detractors are customers that weren't a good fit to begin with.

The other key pillar is creating the right experience and closing the gaps where expectations are unmet through processes and people and service. Sometimes you do need to fix your products or processes, other times you need to fix your message.

From this day forward, it's essential that you start asking the clients who do refer, why they do so. Start asking the clients who don't refer, why they don't. Start asking everyone you do business with what you could do better, and then fix it.

Your goal: a referral number of 100 percent.

You might find some of the resources found at Reichheld's Net Promoter site (netpromoter.com) helpful as you wrestle with the idea of creating and improving your referral number.

Lead conversion for referrals

One of the absolute best places to start a conversation about referrals with a customer is before they actually become a customer. Many businesses take this approach and begin think in terms of referrals as a condition of doing business with the firm. You don't have to state it as such, but this a mind-set that should pervade your entire organization.

If during a sales presentation you're able to state that you know a potential customer is going to be thrilled with the product, service, and experience so much that they are going to want to tell others about it, you accomplish two things: (1) You set the expectation that you are indeed going to check in and make sure they are thrilled, and (2) You are virtually promising them that they are going to be so impressed that they will want to recommend your business. Both are very strong sales messages.

The keys to this process are that you deliver the message in a manner that is consistent with your overall brand, that everyone carries the same message, that you do indeed thrill them, and that you have a process to actually collect referrals—perhaps a planned results-review meeting. The absolute best way to make this a seamless event for all concerned is to make some sort of results review or feedback a routine part of your customer service and sales process. More on that below.

Don't underestimate the power of this concept because it appears very simple. This one idea alone could dramatically impact your outlook on referrals as well as the number of referrals you actually receive from your direct network of customers.

Lifetime value of a customer is unlimited

Maybe you've heard the term some marketers use: "lifetime value." The idea is to calculate what a customer might be worth over the course of doing business in the long term as opposed to over the course of a single transaction. This number might change the way you look at how much you are willing to invest to get each new customer. For businesses that can offer a customer multiple transactions over time, this is a significant concept. For businesses such as home remodelers, who might only work with a customer once in their lifetime, this might not seem to matter.

Here's my take. The lifetime value of every single customer is unlimited when you factor in a customer's ability to make referrals. A logically and emotionally satisfied single-transaction customer might be a source of business for years. In fact, I've personally witnessed a single-transaction customer send substantial amounts of business to a customer of mine over a ten-year period.

So how can this concept inform your marketing approach? In a way, you could take this concept to the extreme and actually give away your products and services to customers, make certain they are pleased, set the expectation for referrals, and never have to go looking for business again.

Could you target customers with significant referral capabilities and test this?

Could you find influencers among your customer base and employ them to try your products and services with the understanding that they use their influence to actively promote your business, not because they received something for free, but because they were able to realize substantial value without risk?

In the spring of 2009 U.S. automaker Ford launched the Fiesta Movement, a grassroots social media campaign to promote the new Fiesta model by placing Fiestas in the hands of one hundred social "agents" and having them promote Ford's new vehicle through Twitter, blogs, video, and events, all without spending a dollar on traditional media. Initial buzz surrounding the initiative was strong as over four thousand people applied to be agents. At the end of the six-month period Ford shared that over fifty thousand people, 97 percent of whom said they had never owned a Ford before, were interested in the car when it became available. As of this writing the cars were not ready to ship, so it's hard to tell if the ultimate objective was met, but it's hard to imagine Ford didn't benefit from the four million–plus views of the YouTube videos associated with the program.

Ben McConnell and Jackie Huba co-authored a fabulous book titled *Creating Customer Evangelists*. In it they recount stories of organizations that do things big and small to turn customers into fanatics who refer their friends, buy your products for others, and willingly provide advice and feedback in an effort to help you get better.

You can also grab a free supplement to the book: *Testify! How Remarkable Organizations are Creating Customer Evangelists* (www .creatingcustomerevangelists.com). This e-book features interviews with companies focused on creating customer evangelists.

Are you easy?

Back in high school being called easy wasn't exactly a compliment, but when it comes to generating referrals from customers, it's essential.

Web folks use the term "frictionless" to describe Web sites that are very simple for the visitor to navigate and experience. There are many places where a business can fall down in this regard, and friction of any kind slows the rate of referral.

So here are some common places to look for friction in your business. Ask yourself, is your business easy:

- to communicate with? Can people contact you or your staff in a number of ways, such as voice mail, e-mail, contact-us page, IM, click to call, click to chat?
- to understand? Do you consistently communicate the description of your narrowly defined market and plaster your simple core message of value on every marketing asset?
- to listen to? Do you have two or three well-developed sales and workshop-type presentations on message?
- to network with? Do you have a give-to-get mentality, do you have a plan to get in front of people online and offline, do you focus on building strategic relationships?
- to trust? Do you consistently produce high-quality, education-based content? Do you keep your promises, do you return phone calls promptly?

- to buy from? Is there a smooth transition once someone agrees to make a purchase? Do you have a delivery and follow-up process, a new customer orientation kit?
- to work with? Engaging experience, results-driven?
- to refer? Tools that teach how to refer, give partners a way to refer, workshops?

I've found one or more of these areas to be gaps in the overall experience for most small businesses. Refer to the customer lifecycle graphic in Chapter 4 or at www.thereferralenginebook.com to help map these actions out.

Customer bill of rights

In 2007, JetBlue had a disastrous week of cancellations and controversies that tarnished the discount airline's reputation and image. Shortly thereafter, in an attempt to regain the trust of their customers, JetBlue introduced something called "The JetBlue Customer Bill of Rights." The idea was to clearly state what customers could and could not expect when it came to departures, cancellations, and even compensation for acts under JetBlue's control.

I've long advocated something I call the "new customer kit" as a tool to orient a customer as to what they can expect and, equally important, what is expected of them. Remember, we are trying to thrill our customers, but in many cases we can't do that unless they participate in their results as well.

Your customer kit bill of rights should contain the following information:

- What to expect from your organization next
- How to contact anyone in your organization with questions
- How to get the most from your new product/service
- What's needed from you to get started
- What was agreed upon today

- How you will be invoiced for work or expected to pay
- How to resolve problems
- Your referral expectations
- Any guarantees
- What they can expect if you don't perform as promised

This isn't meant to be a legal document and a marketing document at the same time, however. If you need an agreement for the sake of legal protection, then you should certainly consult an attorney to create that type of document. One of the primary objectives of your bill of rights is to set the proper expectations and reinforce your marketing messages.

Owner's manual

For some products and services, such as power tools or software, an owner's manual is a very necessary and accepted part of the deal. But many businesses can take this notion to heart and use it as part of their education experience, even if others in your industry don't practice this strategy.

I love it when I buy a product and the first thing I receive is a "getting started" guide, followed by a full tutorial, followed by daily "have you tried this?" e-mails. Every business, product, or service can do the same.

Here are some ideas to get you started:

- Create a getting-started guide for your product, company, or service
- Create a series of how-to videos and promote the links to them in your new customer kit or packing slip
- Create an automated e-mail series that teaches lessons and tips
- Create an online or off-line tutorial session and hold it every Monday at 10:00 A.M. for all new customers. (Make sure everyone in the company can conduct these!)

▶ Create a follow-up phone consultation session as part of your product

It may take a little extra effort initially to create these tools, but the dividends in terms of customer satisfaction and word of mouth will be vast.

I didn't know you did that!

Honestly now: Have you ever heard the words above from a longtime customer? We all have, I'm afraid, and shame on us.

When a customer becomes a customer, it's usually to purchase a specific product or solve a specific problem. When we solve that problem or ship that product, the job is done, right? To build true marketing momentum, the job has just begun.

Above I mentioned creating a new customer kit. This is simply a set of orientation materials that provides your new customer with all the information they need to work with your organization successfully. One of the elements of this kit should be an introduction to all the products and services your company has to offer. That's a good start, of course, but you must do much more than that to drive this information home. When a customer is new to your organization, they may only have one simple need, so you must commit to a long-term process of education as well.

The first thing you should develop is a starter kit to supplement your new customer kit. Depending upon your business, that could be as simple as creating sample packs of other products and shipping them with the original product ordered. A consultant could include executive briefings free of charge to team members or offer an introductory or audit session for other programs.

In addition, I would suggest that you create a monthly introduction process to some aspect of your business and offer this information in several forms. Some examples: a monthly mailing to your entire customer base; a lunch-and-learn with your referral sources; a Web or in-person workshop open to the public; an automated series of educational e-mails for newsletter subscribers, and a permanent post on the company blog.

Keeping all of your products and services featured and top of mind is one of the best ways to do more business with your existing customers and partners. Build this education system, put it on auto-pilot, and you may start hearing, "I'm glad you offer that!"

How to sell anything to anyone

There is a secret to selling more of just about anything to just about anyone, but it's not really about your product or service—the trick is to help them get what they most want.

I know, brilliant in its simplicity, right? Every marketing guru worth their salt tells you to push benefits over features, human desires over product descriptions. The thing is, even this line of thinking stops well short of what I'm talking about, because it's still focused on you and your products. Instead, discover what it is that your customers and prospects want most, and then find ways for your business to help them get that.

An example will help illustrate. If you are an auto dealer, you might think that what people want most is a cool new car. Some people may indeed want that most. They may need that flashy set of wheels to feel better about themselves, but I'm guessing larger numbers really just want a reliable, functional, fairly priced, trustworthy vehicle that, perhaps, feeds their set of values, but mostly does the job.

What those same people *most* want is to fall in love, get a new job, feel better, make more money, have more time, and gain a sense of control in their lives. Heck, it's the human condition. So what if in addition to offering reliable, functional, fairly priced, trustworthy vehicles, you also find ways to make yoga classes, life coaching, gay singles nights, investment how-tos, cooking lessons, and tax preparation part of the way in which you helped people get what they most want, while clearly differentiating your dealership from the pack.

Let's look at a B2B illustration that's near and dear to me. If you're a CPA with small-business customers, what do they most want? Maybe it's to make sense of a balance sheet, but mostly it's to get more customers and get home earlier in the evening. So you've figured out how to tap the Internet and social media to get more customers, and you love playing around with these new tools. Why not help your customers set up a blog, learn how to use Facebook, or optimize their Web sites for local search?

Or, how about building a network of trusted advisers that can help your business customers in many phases of business and systematically bring them together for sessions with your mastermind group of advisers?

When you become a total resource for your customers, when you help them achieve their business and personal goals, you will sell more of anything to anyone. And the best part is, you won't have to sell a thing.

Exceed expectations

Most everyone loves surprises. That's what wrapping paper is all about. Unveiling the unknown and fully appreciating the unexpected. Every now and then it's fun to throw a surprise at your clients and customers as well. This is an area where direct customer contact will serve you well, as the only way to exceed expectations is to first have a sense of what they are.

Here's one of my favorite techniques.

When a customer orders a product or engages your services, toss in something extra. You don't need to make a big deal of it, but do it systematically and don't advertise it. This is one of the easiest ways to overdeliver on expectations.

So let's see:

- When they ask you to prepare their taxes, give them a handy record-keeping system.
- When they order your e-book, send them a copy of your favorite current bestseller from Amazon.
- When they hire you to design a Web site, throw in a blog.

- When they hire you remodel their kitchen, get their windows cleaned.
- When they hire you to install a ceiling fan, change the batteries in their smoke detectors.
- Offer a return policy like Nordstrom's—no time limit, no receipt needed.
- When they order a logo design, give them five hundred business cards from your printing strategic partner.

It's a good practice to make it a surprise (maybe even wrap it like a present), so that it is considered over and above what was expected.

It's amazing how most of life, and certainly most of customer service, is about exceeding or at least meeting expectations. When you make this unexpected gift to your client, you create a great opportunity to communicate the value of all of the services you provide, including this add-on. In some instances companies have created a simple way to exceed expectations, and that simple thing became a key point of differentiation. Enterprise Rent-A-Car broke from the rental car pack by offering to pick customers up at their homes. This point of difference exceeded people's expectations so significantly that it's now the basis of their advertising.

Membership builds loyalty

Coffee shops get it, sub shops get it, even auto maintenance shops get it.

I'm talking about the membership and loyalty club approach to rewarding customers.

Almost any business can add to the bottom line by offering some sort of premium membership option for goods and services that are needed over and over again. The key here is to make an offer that encourages a customer to buy your product more frequently, by offering a discount or the convenience of an automatic shipment. Think book and record clubs, or flower and fruit of the month offerings. Men's Wearhouse has a "shirt of the month" membership program called Fresh Shirt Club that allows members to receive a hand-selected, seasonally appropriate shirt or shirt and tie combo for a set price each month—delivered to your door. Sounds like a great service and an innovative approach for an apparel retailer. I guarantee this moves some shirts.

Southwest Airlines has me as a customer hook, line, and sinker. It starts of course with the fact that they do a better job than any other airline I've experienced at getting you places on time, offering low fares, and allowing you to change flights without hassle, all without charging for checked bags. In addition, they hire the friendliest, most outgoing customer service staff you will ever encounter.

But it's their Rapid Rewards member program that keeps me incredibly loyal. I've taken less than desirable routes and changed my plans so I could fly Southwest, because I earn free drinks and free flights that don't come with any strings attached.

Just about any business can take this approach. In fact, if you offer a core product, you may just want to dream up a service you can offer to support that product and deliver that service routinely. Offer customers a premium "members-only" package or service, or provide value-added events and promotions for members of the club. Send gift certificates or "buy ten, get one free" cards.

Membership breeds loyalty and loyalty breeds referrals.

Beyond vendor

Once you build a little trust with your customers, they often come to rely upon you for more than the scope of your products or services. "I know you're my accountant, but do you know a good estate attorney? My wife and I need to update our wills." Smart providers realize the power in this trust-building advice and actively work to build and develop a network of referable products and services. Some people who practice this strategy become so important a resource for their clients that their clients become virtually locked into the relationship. There is a real estate agent I know who is so good at helping homeowners find great handymen and contractors that her clients don't make a move without calling her first.

Some people are just naturally wired for this, but every business can tap into the power of a network. The key is to go out there and proactively groom your network or resources. Find the "best of class" in a range of products and services that you know your clients may benefit from. Then send letters to each of these providers suggesting that you have clients who could use their services, adding that you would like to know the best way to refer them.

Do this proactively and you will start to build up a network of superstars—all for the benefit of your customers. And a funny thing will happen on the way to building your network: You will begin to receive referrals from your new partners. We'll talk more about this in the next chapter as well.

The ultimate measure of marketing success

While many metrics help marketers determine the success of things like messaging, lead campaigns, and brand awareness, there is one all-important metric that I believe, if captured, is the key to unraveling every marketing challenge that you face.

The measurement that matters over all others is something I've begun calling the customer success quotient (CSQ). In math, a quotient is the result of division. In this case, we are dividing the value you offer by the price you charge. The hope, of course, is that the quotient is positive. In other words, that you offer more in results than you charge to create them. I think initially most people would say they do this, but I wonder. If you're not focused on quantifying the results you create with your customers, it's hard to be certain they are actually receiving or appreciating them.

From a practical standpoint, I believe using and communicating the CSQ as a key marketing indicator in your business does some very powerful things long term.

1. It helps your customers understand the value they are actually receiving. Nothing resells a customer and stimulates referrals like cold, hard results. Sometimes our

customers have short memories; by routinely demonstrating and quantifying the value they receive, you keep results top of mind.

2. It helps you and your staff focus on the one thing that really matters. If every transaction and engagement has a built-in results meter, you can bet people will stay focused on driving the needle as high as possible.

3. It creates a wonderfully compelling marketing story (assuming results are strong). When you can capture and communicate specific results achieved on behalf of your customers, you can offer prospects the kind of proof they need to purchase confidently.

4. It creates the case for dramatically increasing what you charge for your products and services. When you can align the true value of what you do with what you charge, you will unlock the secret to tremendous profits. In fact, this is the key to boldly exploring "fee for results" pricing that can open the door to an entirely new business model for you.

5. The assessment process is one of the best referral-generating opportunities. Creating some sort of results review should be a mandatory part of your overall marketing and customer service routine. This is the ideal place to collect referrals.

In Bob Burg and John David Mann's wonderful book *The Go-Giver* we are introduced to several laws of business. The first is the Law of Value: Give more value than what your product or service costs. While the authors are speaking in terms of giving more in "use" value than the cost, there's no reason this quotient can't be maximized at 1:1.

Every industry and business has to approach this measurement differently, and there are certain types of businesses, such as consulting firms, that can more naturally dive into this way of thinking. The key is to create systems and processes that you know can deliver results, enter only into engagements with customers who value your approach, and set the expectation and process up front for measuring and reporting the results that are achieved.

Do you hold your customers accountable?

Service providers often offer accountability to their customers—at least, that's the promise going in. Your customers often hire you to come in and help, or maybe force, them to do the things they know they should. In some cases, they may actually know how to do what they are asking of you, but they need that extra shove. The question is, at what point are there consequences if customers don't live up to their part of the bargain? At what point do you stop inspiring, cajoling, and yelling, and just start backing off or disengaging altogether? What about building monetary penalties into service agreements that kick in when a customer does not complete assignments they agreed to?

I know this may run counter to the "customer is always right" line of thinking, but I wonder if a customer who won't allow you to do what you were hired to do contributes to the value of your service? At some point they are certain to disengage anyway, and to conclude that your service didn't really help them. Is this any way to build a business?

I was once asked in an interview on this subject about the biggest mistake service providers could make. "Caring more about results than our customers do," I replied. Again, perhaps this sounds a bit cold, but few things will drag you down faster than tethering yourself to a ship this is either sinking or permanently moored. If you are putting yourself out there as a resource to help hold your customers accountable for reaching their goals, achieving a certain level of growth, or reaching a stated objective, then I think you must set very clear expectations that you are going to kick them in the butt or kick them to the curb.

Their success and your reputation may both be at stake if you don't.

Status updates

Communicating with your customers throughout the fulfillment phase of your business is essential. Creating processes that include frequent status updates is a great way to resell your customers, as well as head off any potential snags in the process before it's too late.

Remember, much of the referral game is about meeting and, as often as possible, exceeding expectations, so it's terribly important to manage expectations at all times.

For example, if you manufacture a product, you might:

- communicate when your customer's order goes into production;
- send an update when it's almost finished;
- send a photo before it goes in the box;
- forward a tracking number when it ships;
- call to make sure everything arrived as expected;
- follow-up a week later to make sure all is well.

I took a vehicle into a body shop recently and the shop had cameras mounted in each of the work bays and paint booths. When I brought the car in I was given a URL and access code that allowed me to log in at any time and watch as my car was being worked on. This kind of communication is something that makes people talk, and certainly makes the staff stay focused and accountable.

Staying in touch like this helps build excitement for a purchase, keeps your organization top of mind, and creates many opportunities for word-of-mouth buzz. In many cases, all that's required is a handful of simple processes to enable communication that your competitors wouldn't even dream of.

Ask for bad news, too

Communication is such an essential expectation-meeting tool. One of the most important things you can do is give your customers the opportunity and permission to tell you about the bad stuff as well as the good stuff.

Depending upon which survey you choose to believe, somewhere around 80 to 90 percent of customers who have a bad or misunderstood experience will never tell you about it. This goes for trying to order online, meeting with a salesperson, stumbling through product instructions, or calling customer service. The first line of defense to prevent bad experiences from happening is by making everything as simple, frictionless, and clear as possible. But mistakes are inevitable, and you must encourage people at every turn to let you know what doesn't work.

- Offer lots of ways to easily connect—IM, Twitter, home phone, cell phone, click to call
- Provide feedback forms on your Web site
- Take frequent customer and staff surveys
- Run routine reviews of processes
- Make routine calls to customers to ask how your service is
- Cross-train every member of your staff for every facet of service
- Set up customer review panels and informal customer focus groups
- Offer rewards for pointing out typos and other blunders
- Establish a hard and fast policy of welcoming customer complaints

Some customer complaints are unwarranted and bothersome, but by adopting a policy of encouraging customers to point out any aspect of their experience that's negative, you can head off and fix small problems that might escalate to the point where they dramatically cut into your ability to grow your business.

Don't forget to pay close attention to rating and review directories such as Yelp! and Insider Pages. These directories are designed to help people find local businesses, but they also feature reviews from customers. One bad review can turn potential customers away. By monitoring these sites and proactively recruiting loyal customers to post positive reviews, you can turn these sites into powerful marketing partners.

Staying top of mind

It's an accepted fact that finding ways to do more business or get more referrals from your existing customers is a smart way to build a business. But with all the distractions that capture the attention of a small business, it's easy to forget all about those existing customers until they pick up the phone and reorder.

I advocate creating a calendar of contacts and finding a way to make certain that your customers, referral sources, and hottest prospects never go more than about thirty days without some form of contact. These contacts don't, and in fact shouldn't, always have to be overt sales attempts. I adopted a practice long ago of picking up the phone on Friday afternoons and reaching out to people I felt I hadn't talk with in a while just to see how they were. It rarely fails to turn up some opportunities. Recently, I received a handwritten note from a supplier I have worked with for some time, and it contained a very nice marketing nugget. (I've posted about handwritten notes before. Do them and you will automatically stand out, because nobody writes them anymore.) This particular note was an introduction from a new employee at the organization. It was simply her way of telling me she had joined the company and sharing a little about her background—she wasn't my account rep and she wasn't selling anything.

What a brilliant little tactic. I, the customer, received a contact and was impressed by the handwritten note, and she, the new employee, was allowed to go through and familiarize herself with the organization's entire customer database. Valuable on a bunch of levels.

Reward champions

Every organization that receives any amount of referrals has probably discovered that a disproportionate amount of those referrals come from a handful of customer champions. Of course, these customers are very active in support of your business because they love the experience they've had. But beyond that, these folks are simply wired to make and receive referrals. It's part of who they are, and in many cases it's a big part of what makes them feel good.

Cherish these folks, because they can be responsible for significant amounts of business. In my experience, folks who are wired to be active in this fashion aren't looking for tangible rewards. Your champions are often better rewarded through avenues of appreciation and participation.

In other words:

- Send them flowers, movie passes, and candy with a handwritten note
- Include them in brainstorming and research initiatives
- Host exclusive gatherings where they can meet other advocates
- Introduce them to your strategic partners
- Invite them to events featuring speakers and authors they might enjoy
- Ask for their opinions on business matters
- Include them in your marketing materials
- Let them beta test your new products and services
- Give them free or very low cost opportunities to use your services

These loyal champions should be nurtured and cared for like prized possessions, or they will turn their very important attention and influence where it's more appreciated.

Equipping the team

Making referrals, even for those who aren't your customer champions, should be an easy task. One of the ways you can make referring your products or organization an automatic habit is to equip your customers with lots of tools that make it easy for them to introduce you and your business in logical and tangible ways.

Create a referral toolbox consisting of the following items:

- Personalized referral cards that credit your customer with sending a lead
- Gift certificates with tangible value that a customer can simply hand out
- Trial offers and free evaluations only available through customer referrals
- Customer-exclusive "bring a friend" events online and off-line
- Personalized Web pages that customers can use to educate prospects

The Perfect referral motivation

Do you want to know the best way to motivate referral sources? By now, you've probably realized that it's not money or, for that matter, direct compensation of any form. There will certainly be exceptions of this, but the perfect referral motivation lies in our deep-seated human need for community. People get great pleasure from offering help and knowing they can be called upon as a source of reliable information.

When referral sources are motivated, intentionally or unintentionally, out of a desire to help, they will often go to great lengths to do so. On the other hand, when the motivation is monetary, they will view it as a market transaction, and the motivation is often significantly lower—ranging from indifference to distaste, depending upon the industry. In his fabulous book *Predictably Irrational*, Dan Ariely conducts numerous experiments around the idea of social versus market norms that shed some very tangible light on this idea.

In this brief excerpt from Ariely's book he explains social motivation as I believe it pertains to referrals:

As Margaret Clark, Judson Mills, and Alan Fiske suggested a long time ago, the answer is that we live simultaneously in two different worlds—one where social norms prevail and the other where market norms make the rules. The social norms include the friendly requests that people make of one another. Could you help me move this couch? Could you help me change this tire? Social norms are wrapped up in our social nature and our need for community. The second world, the one governed by market norms, is very different. There's nothing warm and fuzzy about it. The exchanges are sharp-edged: wages, prices, rents, interest, and costs and benefits.

So as a marketer, I believe the message is this: Can you design a referral program that taps into people's desire to help? Can you give them, in a systematic way, the ability to use their influence to add value to the relationship they have with you or with their network?

The highly engaged referral

Not all referrals are created equal. That's not to downplay any referral in any way, but rather to explain that in the conversion from lead to customer, there is one factor that plays a major role.

That factor is the participation of the referral source.

The more engaged your referral source is in the process of making a referral, the more likely it is that the lead will become a customer. The logic is simple: When someone refers a friend to your business, you are ultimately borrowing the know, like, and trust they have built with the referred party. The more engaged they are, the more trust they lend.

From a practical standpoint, you should build participation into your referral process. The more willing your referral source is to participate, the better the lead. Participation can mean picking up the phone and calling a prospect or creating a way to formally introduce your business. In the referral world, a three-way lunch would lie at one end of the spectrum, while a name scribbled on a scrap of paper would lie at the other.

I know someone is doing your business a huge favor by agreeing to make a referral of any sort, but you've got to believe in you heart that you are actually doing them a favor by allowing them to introduce your valuable products and services to others who will benefit. If you can wrap your head around that notion, then you will have no problems devising ways to get your referral sources more engaged.

One urge that you must resist is collecting names from your referral sources and then cold-calling them for a meeting. This is a fabulous way to waste referrals. A referred lead is special—why risk coming off like another telemarketer? Take the time to learn about the referral, and involve your source to the point that you can tailor some special information that lets the lead know they were referred by their good friend.

Referral stories

Just as I urged you to create and use your core marketing story in your branding and strategy development, discussed in Chapter 5, I believe you can also develop and tell powerful stories about the nature and effectiveness of customer referrals.

You may recall that I've suggested that people make referrals for very personal—that's not to say selfish, but rather mutually beneficial—reasons. I make referrals because I like people to know how knowledgeable I am about some things, and because I like to help both parties involved in the process. That's just human nature. I believe marketers can tap into this by capturing and recording referral success stories much like I've suggested you capture and record customer success stories.

In other words, document the benefits a referred party gained because a customer or strategic partner had the foresight to recommend your firm. You don't have to do this in a cold, hard, analytical manner or in a way that might come off as bragging. I believe you can authentically document referral results through simple stories of who, what, when, and how that illustrate the power of referral and the power of results.

Building client and referral communities

Two of the most important words in the marketing world are "content" and "contact." The best lead generation is done by providing tons of great content—and the best lead conversion is done by providing the right kind of contact. Put content and contact together and you not only have a powerful business-building strategy, you have a customer loyalty and referral-generating machine based on connecting people.

Helping people connect in business terms may not be exactly the same as helping teenagers connect online, but the principles bear a striking similarity. The key is to base the community on providing and sharing valuable content and knowledge. The following examples illustrate some easy ways to help prospects and clients gain a deeper connection with your organization:

> **It's just lunch**—I have experienced some pretty fascinating results every time I have brought groups of clients together over lunch. Business owners are starved for contact with their peers—the daily grind makes this just too hard to find. Facilitating this is a great service that any business can offer.
>
> **Peer-to-peer education**—Current clients are probably more prepared to explain the value of youwr service to a prospect, including the limitations. Hold focus groups made up of several existing clients and several prospects. Let the current clients explain, in a nonselling environment, what your service has meant to them, what could be better, and how to get more from it. Sit back and learn.
>
> **Natural word-of-mouth marketing**—When you deepen a relationship with a client by opening up your contacts and clients to them, they will begin to talk naturally with others about what you do that matters to them. You cannot purchase that kind of conversation.

Resource director—Bringing resources together and allowing your clients and prospects to take advantage of those resources is a great way to build community and loyalty. Hosting lunches or even teleseminars with other leading experts is a great example of this type of community building.

Referral communities—What if you put together a group of like-minded businesses, all focused on the same target audience, and you created a local online community, including a blog that each member of the referral group contributed to? This group easily could generate and educate leads in a way that would allow everyone to win. A semiformal referral and comarketing strategy is what you would need to make this take off locally.

Creating client and referral communities is a very satisfying way to build a business. The pressure that some business owners feel from the need to sell is virtually eliminated. Any business or independent professional who takes community building on as a primary marketing strategy, and then sticks with it, can dominate an industry.

Building a community space

Anytime you can gather two or more of your prospects, future prospects, clients, and referral sources there is community building going on. Nothing grows a loyal customer like a connection to something bigger than the product or service you happen to provide.

Not long ago I spoke to a group of retailers and suggested that community building was their greatest weapon against the chain stores. A great way for local merchants to make this concept tangible is to create a physical space and allow the community members (prospects and clients) to use it for PTA meetings, lunches, anniversaries, and fundraisers. You can make the space available for free or charge a token amount; either way, your connection to the community grows. This concept isn't limited to retailers. Any office with meeting space can extend this service to clients and prospects.

Everyone's in customer service

Well, we've gotten to the end of the chapter on creating a positive experience for your direct network of customers, so it should come as no surprise that I'll use this last chunk to remind you that I believe marketing, sales, and customer service falls to everyone in your organization. Sure, there are specific job titles and functions that dictate a person's primary day-to-day duties, but widely referred businesses seem to find ways to empower just about everyone in them to create, deliver, mend, and extend the total customer experience.

The trick is to find ways to balance the necessary "this is how we do it here" process orientation with the "whatever it takes" flexibility that can put a fire out in the early stages.

There's no other way to say this other than—this starts at that top. If the CEO, founder, owner, or chief water buffalo has a customer service mentality, then the entire organization will likely adopt one as well.

Your customer network action plan

What's your referral number?—How will you gauge the level of referral participation present in your customer base?

Lead conversion for referrals—What process will you use to introduce referrals as a condition of doing business with your organization?

Customer bill of rights—How will you communicate what rights and expectations your customer should have as part of a relationship with your firm?

Exceed expectations—What flourishes or surprises can you build systematically into your customer fulfillment processes?

The ultimate measure of marketing success—How will you measure, quantify, and communicate the success or results your customers obtain through your products and services?

Status updates—What mechanisms will you employ to communicate frequent and consistent status updates with your customers?

Reward champions—How will you acknowledge and reward your customer referral champions?

Equipping the team—What tools and processes will you need to build and employ to make it easier for your champions to refer business to your organization?

The highly engaged referral—How can you engage your customers to participate in the referral process at the most personal level?

Everyone's in customer service—What mechanisms, training, and mind-set is necessary to ensure that everyone in the organization is delivering customer service in line with the overall brand strategy?

CHAPTER 9

The Strategic Partner Network

Far too often marketers focus the bulk of their referral energy on their existing customer base. The rationale behind this is sound—after all, this group has experienced your brilliance firsthand and should be able to easily and authentically tell their referral story to others in need.

This is the logic we applied in the previous chapter to your customer referral network. But now I want to turn the attention to another, often underappreciated group I call your strategic partner network.

In simplest terms, this is a group of business owners who share your description of an ideal customer. In other words, businesses that sell to your customers and prospects. This network quite often can possess far greater referral opportunities if for no other reason than sheer numbers. A happy customer might know three or four ideal referrals, but a large, indirect network partner may have the trust of several hundred.

In addition, partner network members usually have a stronger motivation to act on your behalf. In most cases, a referral is made by a customer because they bump into someone who needs what you do. Strategic partners may find that it makes sense for them to actively promote your business or solution as a way to increase the value of the relationship they have with their customer base.

In this chapter I am going to present a very specific course of action to help you identify, groom, and activate your indirect network.

Constructing your value networks

At this point it should come as no surprise that the act of building your network is very much an inbound one. You can use the exact same principles about being found over hunting to identify and activate your indirect network.

The first key to building a powerful referral network is to adopt the proper point of view—in this case, the point of view of your customer. As you identify and recruit members to be part of your indirect team, you should always filter your list based on this question: "Would I feel 100 percent confident referring my best customer to this business?" If a potential strategic or referral partner can't pass that test, then don't even consider entering into a referral relationship.

If you adopt that mind-set you will never attempt to add a referral partner based simply on what you think they can do for you—and that distinction is huge. If you always ask yourself what a potential relationship might mean for your customer, you will most likely stay on the right track.

One of the most powerful things you can do to increase your value in the eyes of your customers is to become a wealth of information and resources related to all of your customer's needs, even if they may be unrelated to what you sell or provide. If you or your business can become known as the go-to provider for any need under the sun, you can develop a very important place in the mind of your customer.

There are many ways to build your list of potential strategic network members, and in many cases you might want to develop two distinct lists. The first is what you might normally call strategic members. These are people or businesses that have your same ideal customer in their sights. For example, an accountant and an attorney are commonly paired as strategic partners. Each can make introductions at what might be seen as a peer-to-peer level. Referrals with strategic members are almost always seen as a mutually beneficial interaction.

The second list I advise every business to develop is a list of what might be called provider members. In many cases provider members don't interact with or have the ability to introduce strategic relationships, but they provide necessary products and services, and can prove very beneficial as a means to help offer "best of class" products and solutions or to step in and help a referred business that isn't really a good match for you.

If you've ever received a call from someone who was referred to you by a good customer but isn't a match for you, having to say "no, we don't do that" isn't a satisfying resolution for everyone concerned. However, with a ready group of supplier members who *do* do that, you can refer these people along to the right source. Everyone wins.

This group doesn't provide referrals to your organization, mainly because in their businesses they don't interact with your ultimate target, say, the CEO or VP of marketing, but they can be very helpful in collaboration roles and as a value-added way for you to help your customers get what they need.

Identifying your strategic team

It bears repeating that it's crucial to view your referral partners first and foremost as those you would refer your best customers to. If that is the case, you must take some time to craft your list based on feedback from numerous sources as well as on your own research.

For your strategic list, you certainly want to start with those businesses or individuals about which you already have a working knowledge. These can be businesses that you already use, such as your bank or attorney, or businesses that you have collaborated with in a joint venture. You should also consider adding members to this list based on their reputation in the market, even if you don't currently have a working relationship of any kind. (I'll show you how to engage this group later on in this chapter.)

Finally, you want to round out your strategic and provider lists by asking your current strategic partners, vendors, staff, and customers for their best-of-class suggestions for every category of product or service they care to share. Frequently, when I've employed this strategy, some names come up time and again, making them a sure bet for your prospecting list. Having a conversation with your customers about the fact that you are building a referral network including some of their favorite providers is in and of itself a strong marketing and loyalty message.

Lastly, don't discount organizations you may think of as competitors.

A Canadian marketing consultant, Kris Bovay (www.more-for-small-business.com), shared her success with this idea:

> In our region, a number of large companies regularly put out requests for proposal (RFPs) and, unfortunately, my small business had been unsuccessful in winning any bids that we submitted. This was somewhat demoralizing and frustrating, particularly because RFPs often take quite some time to produce.
>
> At an industry association meeting, I met up with one of my competitors and chatted about business in general in our province (we're in BC [British Columbia], Canada). We somehow transitioned into talking about RFPs and commiserating with each other about how both of our companies had trouble "winning" bids. One thing led to another, and we agreed that the next bid would be a joint affair. The combination of both of our businesses, our experiences, our access to staff (most of our "staff" are contract consultants) helped us to win the next joint bid we submitted in response to a request for proposal for a strategic business plan update. And that joint bid led to others. This relationship started about one year ago. We've worked together on 3 projects; we've submitted 5 joint bids. Our "win" rate has gone up from zero!
>
> We did put some "rules" in place: we defined who was responsible for what; we have taken turns on who's the contractor and who's the sub; we have developed a template for the joint applications; etc. I'd certainly recommend doing this if you know, and trust, the individual—for example, I wouldn't have done this if I didn't like and respect this individual as a competitor.

Invitation to join

The goal of creating the lists above is the eventual creation of a network of strategic and provider partners. This network will become a central element of your marketing and customers service efforts moving forward. Depending upon your business model, this network can be as formal or as casual as you like, but building it with the intention of offering added value to your customer base is essential.

Once you have your list of prospective network members, you will need to develop an introduction process. I have used a very specific process for network building for many years, and it never fails to pique the interest of anyone who I have engaged using it. The cornerstone of this process is to inform the provider that I "have customers who may need the products or services their firm offers," adding that I "would like to know more about how to best introduce them." You may also want to specifically refer to the customer who recommended them.

Craft a letter of introduction spelling out your desire to learn more about their business and send this to every member on your list.

Make it easy for your network contact to teach you about their business. I've developed a simple form that asks them to answer the following questions:

1. How would I spot your ideal customer?
2. How would I best describe your unique benefits, approach, products, services, or value proposition?
3. What might prospects say to trigger me to know they need to be referred to you?
4. What is your marketing process once you receive a referral?

This simple four-question survey can go a very long way toward helping you to get to know more about your partners. To make it even easier for them to complete it, go ahead and add a completed one for your own business. This will both show prospective partners how best to answer the questions and indirectly provide them with information about your business.

The impact of this process is usually immediate, as many of the recipients will view it as an invitation to contact you to learn more. Take the time to meet, follow up, and discover all that you can about any of the folks who show an interest. This getting to know you period is not about yielding business referrals; it's about developing a relationship and exploring ways to work together.

How to activate your network

Once you have developed a working understanding with a number of strategic partners, you'll want to help them understand how you can benefit each other. I find that many business owners have great intentions when it comes to partnering, but the trick always lies in trying to figure out how to make logical introductions to customers without doing so in a forced or unnatural manner.

This is where much of the content creation we discussed back in Chapter 6 will come to your aid.

Even though many businesses have learned the importance developing valuable educational content in the form of white papers, e-books, and workshops, it can be a lot of work. It can also pay big dividends, but the up-front investment of time can be a very real roadblock. Another great incentive to get you past this initial hurdle is that this content can be used as a powerful door-opening solution for partnering. You can use your free reports and valuable workshops with strategic partner prospects as a ready-made introduction and partnering method.

Below are several proven methods for creating compelling partnering opportunities.

Cobranding

Let's say you're a business consultant and you've created a twelve-page report called "Top 10 Tips for Squeezing More Profit from Your Business." You know that your customers and prospects find this bit of information very useful. In fact, many of your current customers first came to know about your expertise by consuming this very report.

When you begin conversations with members of your indirect network about ways to work together, offer your very effective little marketing report for them to distribute to their customers—they can even cobrand it by adding their logo and contact information. Now that's an offer that's hard to turn down, and it presents a very natural way for this partner to introduce you to their entire database of customers with very little effort and great mutual benefit.

The primary reason this approach is so effective is because you've done all the work and have even presented the idea. In some cases you will be courting the attention of very influential partners, ones that get lots of requests for partnering or referral relationships. By suggesting a campaign that is very easy to employ, you'll rise to the top of the list.

Workshops

You have the option of choosing from a number of creative approaches when considering how to activate your strategic network via some form of presented content.

The first approach is very similar to the cobranded free-report tactic but with a workshop or seminar as the branded element. Workshops are simply another form of content, ones with the added trust-building benefit of personal interaction. This format has provided great benefits, since it gives companies the ability to present to groups large and small via Web technology.

As I stated in Chapter 6, I believe every business, no matter the industry or product, should develop at least one killer educational presentation that both gives people info on something they want to know more about and demonstrates that you or your organization has something important to say. Don't write this off because you don't feel like a good speaker; people want the information. If it's good enough, the rest comes down to style. On the other hand, don't coast on your natural speaking talents with a thinly disguised marketing pitch. Content that has value must come first.

Once you have created and refined your workshop, you're ready to take it to your strategic partners and offer to provide this great information as a value-added service to their customers. Make clear that this isn't a sales pitch but rather a great informational session. You may want to create a video of the actual presentation along with a transcript. Sell the value of the content by explaining the benefit to their customers.

Combined workshop. Several other implementations of the workshop as partnering strategy include working with more than one partner at a time. For example, you can approach two partners and suggest the workshop be held as a joint presentation for the benefit of both partners. This way they get to offer this valuable content to their customers and meet each other's customers with the prospect of potential new business and you are ushered in as the expert and get exposure to the entire audience of participants. The right partners can make this a very powerful approach.

Another way to employ workshops is to suggest an event held by three or four partners, including you. In this format, each partner presents information related to their area of expertise. Each partner is also responsible for inviting their customers and contacts for this half- or full-day event. This kind of event can create a very high perceived value and effectively creates referral introductions for all who participate.

Cocreate content

Technology has made it very easy to create multimedia content. You can engage partners to create new content with you quickly by simply conducting and recording audio or video interviews on subjects of interest to your prospects and customers. In the span of twenty minutes you may be able to capture the essence of a solution to problems your customers routinely face. You can methodically work your way through your entire strategic network suggesting topics and capturing very valuable information. You can use the suggestion of these interviews as a great way to initiate a strategic relationship and the end product as a great way to introduce your partners to your customers and further solidify your place in your partner's mind.

Joint marketing

Another very powerful way to activate your network is to devise ways that each partner can market each other in either passive or active ways.

For example, I once worked with an electrical contractor who had developed joint marketing relationships with a plumber and with a heating-and-cooling company. Each of the three partners distributed each other's marketing materials and coupons with each service call and in routine mailings.

You can also recruit a team of partners to give you high-value samples or trial products to pair with your core offerings as a way to differentiate and sweeten the deal. There are hundreds of high-quality partners that would love the introduction to your customers. Here's an example: A graphic designer can partner with online printers such as UPrint or VistaPrint to give five hundred free business cards to each of the design firm's logo customers. Now the design firm has something to add a little spice to their marketing message. (They can also create an affiliate relationship with the print shop for additional purchases.) In this example, the print shop wins because they have very little real cost in the business card printing and, let's face it, won't that business get new stationery and other printed items with that new logo on it?

How you construct this tactic depends upon your industry and the way you communicate with your customers and prospects. Think in terms of the online model. Many online companies offer thirty- to sixty-day free trials. Take this idea out to businesses in your community and start putting together a package of products and services that turn prospects' heads.

Some idea starters:

- Be the electrician who gives your customers a free AC checkup and one free drain cleaning
- Be the marketing consultant who offers a free product-trademark review with an IP attorney
- Be the accountant who gives your customers a free IT and computer network audit

- Be the retail store that gives ten-minute massages to weary shoppers

Are you starting to get some ideas on how you might attack this? Don't stop at one pairing; go for several ways that enhance and differentiate your products and services by adding real value from willing partners.

The odd couple

As we've discussed at length already in this chapter, creating the right partnership or two can create an instant and steady flow of leads. But what I really like, because it can create more buzz than the typical, logical relationships, is when a couple of businesses that you don't normally think of as partners find a creative way to benefit each other mutually.

For example:

- I was staying in Estes Park, Colorado, once and stopped at Coffee on the Rocks, which offered free fly-casting lessons every day out on the stream that ran behind the store. The coffee shop received business each day as families came in to get the free lesson. The lesson was held by a local fishing shop that also signed up participants each day for their guided fishing tours. (The coffee shop owner told me that some people come in just to watch!)
- An IT consulting firm wanted to partner with CPAs at large firms. To get their attention, it brought in massage therapists—the CPAs were treated to a back massage as they listened to the presentation. Not only did the IT firm stand out and get the attention of the sometimes reluctant CPAs, but the massage business acquired new customers.

The fully engaged network

Once you've developed a bit of a rhythm with a base group of strategic partners, it may be time to take it up a notch and create a more formal structure that includes not only many of the tactics discussed above, but also a more public promotion of your network and its members.

A great way to way to create a public platform for your network is to use a blog featuring contributions from each of its members. With a number of business specialties represented and authors sharing the workload, this tactic shouldn't be too much of a chore for any one partner. Since you should substantially share the same ideal target customer, your collective efforts will produce a content hub that prospects and search engines will find very useful.

The exposure your online network hub offers to its contributors can be positioned as yet another benefit of becoming a part of your network. If all of the members are local businesses targeting local prospects, the local search engine value of this strategy alone makes it worth the effort.

Teach your network well

If you want your strategic partners to generate referrals for your business, teach them how to generate more referrals for their own. In addition to educating your strategic partners on the basics—how to spot your ideal customer, how to present your core difference, what prospects say that trigger referrals, and what your referral marketing process is—you should proactively teach your strategic partners how to use many of the tools and ideas suggested in this book.

In fact, some of the first seminars you should offer to your strategic network is one that teaches them how to create larger, more engaged networks, how to create and offer cobranded content and workshops, and perhaps even how to create their own blog network as an advanced strategic partner benefit.

The net effect of all this teaching is that you and your business will enjoy some of the fruits of your students' successes while further cementing a referral culture and reputation.

Make-a-Referral Monday

To drive the message of referral marketing home in your business, designate Referral Mondays. On Mondays, every member of the organization's stated and charted goal is to refer someone to another business. These referrals can go to strategic partners or to your uncle Louie's catering business, as long as you can match someone in need with a best-of-class solution. You can take your efforts out into the world and advertise and recruit others to join in. Post your Make-a-Referral Monday initiative in your newsletter, on your blog, and through social networks such as Twitter.

There is a popular way people categorize and group things on Twitter, using something called a "hashtag." It's nothing more than including the # symbol and any other text. People can search and find other tweets using the same tag. A very popular one is called Follow Friday: People suggest other users they consider worth following and add the tag #FF or #followfriday. This way, people can find lots of users to follow by searching on those tags. Readers of this book can start a new tag for Make a Referral Monday (#marmon). Get your entire universe of prospects, customers, vendors, partners, competitors, mentors, and staff involved, and make it a game.

I can think of few things that would create a culture of referral buzz more quickly and authentically than a public campaign of making referrals.

Your partner network action plan

Identifying your strategic partner prospects—Who belongs on your strategic partner team, and how will you identify more?

Invitation to join—What process will you employ to help strategic partners view working with you as a direct benefit to them?

How to activate your network—What content cobranding, workshop, joint marketing, or creative partnership ideas will you employ to get your network active?

The fully engaged network—How will you structure and fully promote a more formal group of partners?

Teach your network well—What tools and tactics will you employ to teach your network partners how to be better referral marketers and generate more referrals for themselves?

Make-a-Referral Monday—What tactics can you devise to keep the focus on giving referrals for everyone in your indirect network?

CHAPTER 10

Ready to Receive

In a way we've come full circle in the world of the widely referred business.

So far I've asked you to build a substantial marketing and referral strategy and foundation and to fortify it with a hub of content that educates. Further, you've practiced, or at least are motivated to practice, the art of blending online and off-line marketing tactics for maximum leverage.

All that's left at this point is to receive more referrals. Of course, there's a bit of an art to receiving a referral.

How to frame a referral request

There will always be some reluctance in asking for referrals.

One of the keys to becoming a Referral Engine—in fact, the key to any marketing message—is to frame it as a benefit. When you are talking to an existing client, the benefit of a referral is the opportunity to help that person help a friend or raise their perceived value with a colleague. Ask yourself: How could referring your business make your client's life better? That's the proper way to think about referrals. Do that, and you will never be afraid to ask a client again.

Remember, you are not asking your clients for help—you are offering to help them get more of what they want. Use your expertise to make them look good, add value, and enhance their status.

Now that's a winning proposition.

When to ask

There are certain tried-and-true opportunities available to the widely referred business that suggest a referral is in order. The key is to recognize, be ready, and take full advantage when those opportunities present themselves.

We've covered the notion of building referral expectation into your lead-conversion process and building systems that allow you to collect referrals consistently. There are creative opportunities, however, for spur-of-the-moment referral situations.

In my experience you should be ready to ask for a referral under the following conditions:

- A customer voluntarily suggests that your product or service is "incredible"
- When a customer sends an unsolicited testimonial
- When a customer refers someone—that's right, now is the time to ask for more
- When a customer admits you've saved their rear end
- When a strategic partner tells you about an association they've joined
- When you complete a project with a customer

Really, the only time not to ask for a referral is during the process of making one yourself—keep these two acts separate or you run the risk of muddying your motivations.

What a referral can tell you

Referrals are great—especially when they quickly turn into a highly qualified, ideal client.

That's the real promise of a referred prospect, isn't it? They've been made aware of you, told why they should like you, and shown what you do that is different, valuable, and trustworthy. So here's a little tip: The next time someone calls you up and says, "My friend said I should contact you," I want you to immediately call the referral source up and ask them why they did so. You may have an idea, but it's the actual words, while they still remember, that are important. We go through life thinking we know what the client values about our business, but it's often not what we think it is.

Schloegel Design Remodel (www.remodelagain.com/Schloegel _Design_Remodel/Home.html), a remodeling contractor located in Kansas City, Missouri, wanted to find out what their past customers valued most about working with them. They did very high-end work and assumed that most customers appreciated their quality craftsmanship. They were right, of course—their customers did appreciate their quality and attention to detail. But what they appreciated most was that the crews cleaned up the job site every night before they went home. The distinction allowed them to focus more narrowly on why people referred them.

When someone goes to the trouble to refer a friend or colleague, there is a good chance they have a reason you should hear about. So, ask already: What makes you want to refer us? What do we do that's unique? What do people say that makes you think of telling them about us? If you can capture some of this from a motivated referral source, you may find clues to a simple core message you should be using in all of your marketing.

And there's always a flip side—you may discover that your referral sources don't really know what you do well or are communicating what you do incorrectly.

Now you can go to work on fixing that.

How to give a referral

I've written at length about the need to give referrals as a component of the ability to receive them, and as such I believe there's an effective way to give a referral. Always start with the right mind-set, and that's a mind-set of getting the referred lead what they need, as opposed to making a sale and getting more of what you need for yourself.

With that in mind, I suggest that you stay as involved as possible in the process. You strengthen the referral process when you can stay a part of it long enough to ensure that value is obtained by all. If you can, make personal introductions and check in with your referred lead to see if they achieved the results they were seeking. When you simply toss a customer to another supplier, either because they weren't a good fit for you or because you don't provide what they were seeking, you forfeit the opportunity to create direct value for the customer or the prospect and miss an opportunity for building a bridge to the potential long term value of giving referrals without regard to future compensation.

I have experienced firsthand the impact of genuinely guiding a lead that wasn't a fit for me to another, more appropriate source and then to receive referrals because they felt I did the right thing in helping them. It's easy to qualify a lead and quickly determine they aren't worth your time, but if you take the time to find the right value for every referred lead, the payoff will be momentum.

Involve your employees in the referral machine

There are lots of great ways to systematically stoke the Referral Engine, but an often overlooked one is the engagement of your entire staff. Every employee, marketing-related function or not, should be brought into the referral game and motivated, empowered, and rewarded for playing the game to win.

Here's how:

> **Help fill your gaps**—If you are not automatically receiving a flood of referrals it may be due to the fact that some of your processes are leaking—customers are not receiving an experience that connects them with your brand emotionally. Challenge your employees to come up with ways to turn every customer contact, even financial and operational ones, into touch points for referrals.

Make referrals daily—Build your network of select strategic partners and encourage employees to make referrals to those partners when they can. Create a bonus
point pool for making referrals. Make giving referrals a
business strategy.

Automate customer testimonials—So often your frontline employees are standing there when the customers
sighs and says, "Wow, dude, you really saved my butt on
this one." Alert: This is a great time to get a customer
testimonial. Start offering bonus points for every testimonial acquired by every employee. This one could turn
into a pretty fun game for the entire staff.

Offer employees referral bonuses—This one is pretty
straightforward, but sometimes the obvious still applies.
Incentivize every employee to generate word-of-mouth
buzz and create referrals that turn into customers.

Don't stop at a referred prospect, though. Go way beyond that to
referred new employees, referred strategic partners, referred buddy
down at the newspaper, and referred genius tech gal that can automate
stuff you are still doing manually.

Put one or all of the above in place and watch the mind-set at your
business make a major shift. Everybody's in marketing, no matter what
the org chart says!

Using technology to nurture leads

Lead nurturing is the act of following up in a consistent and logical
way, moving them gently along the path to becoming a customer. In
some high-end, long-decision-process selling environments, such as an
enterprise-wide software installation or expensive capital goods purchase, it's the only way a sale is made. "Hi, Susie said you need help,
call me when you're ready to buy," isn't a very nurturing approach.

A referred lead comes with a trickier sales cycle than a lead generated, let's say, through an ad campaign. Tricky because in some

environments a referred lead might come beating your door down wanting to know how they can get what their friends down at Consolidated Plumbing got. In other environments they might not have even fully accepted that they have the problem or need that is so painfully obvious to the accountant who referred them to you.

It's essential to build follow-up routines that help you meet various sales and education cycles while still moving these leads along the path to becoming customers. This is a place where technology shines.

In some cases it's a matter of employing a technological solution to drip more and more information to a referred prospect automatically, and to monitor what e-mails are opened, what links are clicked, and how much time is spent on a Web page. Employing these technologies can help you know exactly when your prospect is showing interest. (Don't worry, none of this needs to be done in a creepy way; it's all a matter of using technology to gather the information your prospects are willing to share.)

The secret is to stay top of mind and continue to educate in ways that have impact.

The following list of tools are valuable to any small business owner to use for lead nurturing in tandem with a reserve of educational content.

> **BatchBook**—(www.batchblue.com) is a lightweight CRM tool with a twist. BatchBook makes it very simple to add your prospects' social media profiles, thereby having access to their blog and Twitter feeds right at the point of interaction. Observing what a referred prospect tweets or writes on their blog over time can give you or the salesperson you assigned to the lead tremendous insight into what they care most about. This is the kind of research any sharp salesperson does anyway—but now it's a lot easier! This is also a good way to keep up on your target journalists too.
>
> **ACT!**—(www.act.com) is the granddaddy of desktop CRM software. ACT! allows you to set up "campaigns," which can be many things, but when it comes to referral

follow-up the most effective use is to create a series of follow-up letters that are triggered over time by the addition of a prospect to your referral campaign. You can create branches, too, so that if a prospect attends an event or participates in a sales presentation you can move them to a different message track. ACT! also allows you to follow your contacts' social media activities inside each record.

Infusionsoft—(www.infusionsoft.com) is a hybrid CRM, e-mail, shopping cart, and affiliate tool all rolled into one. It's not for every business, but if you have large lists to manage and want a really great tool for segmenting and targeting various types of referral lists, this is a great tool.

Swiftpage—(www.swiftpage.com) is an e-mail add-on tool that allows you to e-mail one or many referral prospects and then receive ranking reports based on how the prospect interacted with the message. Swiftpage integrates with ACT! and Outlook and helps you understand your prospect's level of interest, so you can plan your follow-up accordingly.

AWeber—(www.aweber.com) is a low cost but very effective autoresponder and e-mail service. An autoresponder is a tool that allows you to create an e-mail or a series of e-mails that are automatically delivered to a prospect when they fill out a form or request a follow-up. The nice thing is that you can set these to deliver over long periods of time. Autoresponders have been around for some time now, but they are still a very effective way to drip information to prospects via e-mail.

SendPepper—(www.sendpepper.com) is an autoresponder that adds direct mail. When a prospect is referred to your Web site and fills out a form requesting more information, they receive an auto e-mail message right away and a high-impact postcard a few days later. The postcard offers the prospect a URL (prospectname.yoursite.com) that sends them to a personalized landing page to receive more details created just for them.

This level of personalization, even through technology, adds to the message that your referred lead is unique.

Web conferencing—services such as Glance, iLinc, Go-ToWebinar, or WebEx give you the ability to offer your referred prospects the opportunity to attend demos, peer2peer panels, collaboration sessions, or even sales presentations from the comfort of their offices. You can also record and archive your Web conferences to offer in other formats.

Handwritten notes—are the ultimate low-tech, high-touch tools and still the greatest lead- and referral-nurturing tools around. Get in the habit of sending a dozen or so a week, and you'll be hooked forever.

By employing one or more of the tools listed above in an effort to slowly and logically educate your referred prospects, easily stay top of mind, and proactively move to lead conversion at precisely the right time, you referral efforts will systematically convert a much high percentage of referred leads into paying customers.

Fix the follow-up

Systematic follow-up is probably the one of the most unheralded secrets to marketing success, but done well, it's the catalyst to long-term referral momentum. There are a number of tactical follow-up steps that, if practiced routinely, add depth to the level of engagement required to build sustainable marketing momentum.

What a referred lead needs to know

Far too many businesses blend all their leads together in one follow-up path. A referral is a lead, true, but (for the many reasons we've covered), it's a very special kind of lead and deserves an exceptional follow-up. You don't need to design an entirely separate set of lead-conversion processes, but you do need to change the way you build know, like, and trust. The logical order of things has been upset a bit when a lead is referred. To some degree they may trust you without knowing or liking you.

If you assume that that means you don't need to take special care in building know and like, you are very mistaken. In fact, that's what gets people in trouble with referred leads—there is an assumption that since "Joe said I should call you," the true value of that you have to offer has been understood fully. But you still need to educate the lead about your expertise and demonstrate your wonderful process. The only difference is that you may have a more attentive audience because of the relationship they have with your referral source. Of course, that additional trust also comes with the expectation that they will receive special attention. And rightly so.

I've found that two simple processes can go a very long way toward meeting the requirements of this tactic.

- **Acknowledge that you are working with a special lead.** Tell the lead, on first contact, either in person or by way of an automated technical follow-up path, that they were referred by X.
- **Let them know that because they were referred you have something unique for them.** This can be free information, an evaluation, a book, a box of chocolates—to some degree what it is is not as important as the fact that you are affording your lead a special status due to their relationship with your referral source.

What a referral source needs to know

Your referral sources need to know a thing or two as well. In fact, the more you communicate with your referral sources, the more qualified and abundant your referrals will grow, and the more motivated your referral sources will be to act.

The very first thing your referral sources need to know is that you respect the trust they are loaning you and that you never intend to break that trust through aggressive selling or poor service.

Previously in this book we covered, in some detail, the proper way to educate your referral sources as part of your referral system, but in reference to this discussion on follow-up it never hurts to reiterate your marketing process to your referral sources—in other words, tell them exactly what your team does when a lead is referred to your business. This includes the two-step process above.

If a lead is not right for your business, don't just ignore it; use it as an opportunity to explain more thoroughly the ideal referral your business is looking for. You may have to tread cautiously during a conversation like this, but I've found that an honest discussion here can head off potential misunderstandings that can come from either seeming unresponsive or, worse yet, trying to help someone you're not really set up to help. In the latter case you may actually damage your relationship with your referral source.

Lastly, no matter what kind of referrals you receive from your referral sources, you must make it a habit of expressing your appreciation. If you've created a business that people want to talk about, they will do it voluntarily, but there's something particularly motivating about knowing that their efforts are genuinely appreciated. There are countless ways to do this. One of my favorites is to send flowers, but you may also discover a unique interest or enjoyment that your referral source has and use that to inform your appreciation sharing.

Acknowledge every phase

Another important element in the follow-up routine is to acknowledge the various types of referrals in different manners. Depending upon your particular business, you may have referral sources that send you many qualified referrals before you ever turn one of them into a profitable customer.

It's as important to acknowledge the sent referral as it is to acknowledge the converted referral. This keeps the tap flowing while you work your leads in an effort to turn them into customers. If you only say thanks for the ones you close, you will find that your referral sources will feel unappreciated before that ever occurs.

You may want to send some movie tickets or even a handwritten thank-you to acknowledge a referral of any sort, and then devise ways to show a different level of appreciation for a lead that becomes a cus-tomer. Remember, this is a thank-you for a nice deed, something unex-pected, and not a financial business transaction. The difference is night and day when it comes to developing the proper motivation.

Communicate the progress

Another form of follow-up that further involves and motivates your refer-ral sources is to keep them in the loop with regard to referrals they've made. This can be as simple as letting them know by e-mail that Bob decided to join or to go with a competitor. Or, it can be far more specific with regard to an actual result you helped Bob achieve. (Obviously there are privacy issues to consider with this tactic, but few things reinforce referrals more than proof that a positive outcome was achieved.)

This is a step that needs to be intentionally written into your referral plan or you run the risk of accomplishing it in a hit-or-miss fashion only.

Thank publicly

Where appropriate, acknowledging your referral source's activity on your behalf publicly can be a powerful motivator. Almost everyone enjoys a little pat on the back for being a part of the team, and I believe doing this in the right forum has several benefits.

- Your referral sources feels appreciated
- You reinforce your organization's referral worthiness
- You display tangible examples of referral partners

The flip side of this idea is that you also refer publicly as part of the entire cycle. By letting people know the kinds of businesses you deem referral-worthy you:

- demonstrate what you think represents quality by those you associate with;

- provide more leads for your referral partners through public promotion;
- share resources that benefit your customers and prospects;
- demonstrate how highly you value referrals by giving the idea such prominence.

There are many ways you can go about promoting your referral activity publicly. You can add a referral box to your newsletter, create a referral news page on your Web site, promote referrals in your blog posts, or tweet it to your followers on Twitter.

Your ready-to-receive action plan

How to frame a referral request—How will you position your requests for referral in a manner that offers your referral source the benefit of doing so?

What a referral can tell you—What process will you create to ensure that you understand why each referral source recommends your organization?

How to give a referral—What process will you create to ensure that you are making referrals as effectively as you are receiving them?

Involve your employees in the Referral Engine—How can you get every employee involved in the acquisition of referrals?

Fix the follow-up—What processes will you need to create to properly and effectively follow up with your referred leads and your referral sources?

Communicate the progress—How will you track, capture, and communicate the progress and results you achieve on behalf of your referred leads?

Thank publicly—What tools and processes will you utilize to acknowledge and appreciate your referral sources?

CHAPTER 11

Referral-specific Campaigns

Over the course of my years writing and speaking about marketing and referrals, I've received hundreds of cards, letters, examples, and e-mails from smart marketers out there making some of the very tactical ideas presented in this book work for them. In this chapter I am going to share what I think are some really great ideas sent directly to me from readers. Each of the ideas supports at least one of the concepts presented throughout the book, and it's my hope that these real-world examples will help to further illustrate some ideas presented already.

Two fine referral examples

There are a handful of referral offers that are based on simple foundations proven successful for years. I preach the creative use of these all of the time, so it's always nice when I come across businesses utilizing them. I would like to share two examples, one focused on a direct network member and the other on an indirect strategic partner base.

The first one comes from Omaha Steaks (www.OmahaSteaks.com). This longtime mail-order meat shipper has always been recognized as an innovative marketer, particularly in the direct-mail world. The offer they are making comes under the gift certificate category offer. Essentially what this type of offer does is give a gift to a customer and ask them to share it with friends (referrals)—the offer further incentivizes the source by allowing them to earn points, money, prizes, etc., when those referred become customers. The Internet has certainly made running a program like this much easier.

The key is giving the gift to your referral source, so they have something tangible and valuable that they can use to give away to make the referral happen.

Here's their pitch:

> Invite your friends to try Omaha Steaks and we'll throw in a dozen free burgers. And for every two friends who try us out, we'll send you a $20 Reward e-Gift Card towards your next purchase of $80 or more.

They run the entire campaign with a landing page at shareomaha steaks.com and use snail mail and e-mail to push traffic to the page. According to a case study prepared by the company's direct mail agency, Johnson Direct, in one of the first months of the program, we were able to boost the average order size by 7 percent.

The second example comes from VerticalResponse (www.Vertical Response.com), an e-mail marketing service provider in San Francisco, whose CEO, Janine Popick, you met early on in this book.

The Vertical Response offer, focused on generating referrals from partners, falls into the cobranding category. For this kind of offer you simply create valuable educational content and package it in the form of an e-book, white paper, webinar, or seminar and take it to partners and let them cobrand (put their logo and contact info on) the content and use it with their customer base.

The appeal of this approach is that everyone knows that they should be producing this kind of content, but who has the time? By bringing your partners an out-of-the-box solution you make yourself easy to partner with and promote—and that is one of the keys to any referral-partner relationship.

Vertical Response produced a report, "10 Marketing Resolutions for the New Year," and offered it to its affiliate partners complete with the partner's logo.

I teach these types of approaches, but nothing illustrates a point like a tangible example. Employing multiple referral programs, focused on different market segments and partners, is the key to building a culture of referral.

Exchanging services for advertising

Large advertisers have been doing it for years—"Buy our product and get a free T-shirt to help spread the word about our company."

I love this type of grassroots promotion, and I think small businesses underestimate how a well-run promotion involving every customer can turn into a flood of buzz and referrals.

Employees at Jobing.com (www.Jobing.com), headquartered in Phoenix, have the option of getting their cars wrapped in the company's advertisement in exchange for five hundred dollars a month in free gas. This is just a twist on the age-old endorsement tactic, but by doing all the work for your customer, creating the bumper sticker and offering an incentive, you get immediate benefits. Cars are a great vehicle because they move around like minibillboards, but so do pizza boxes, flower arrangements, real estate signs, backpacks, and bikes.

The key is to offer an incentive that makes people talk—free oil changes for life can do that. Make the incentive about your products and services so you can continue the relationship with your client and highlight a feature of your business that they may not be as familiar with.

A nonprofit partnership referral model

I interviewed Eric Groves, senior VP of sales and development of ConstantContact, one of the leading e-mail marketing service providers. During our visit, he shared with me some information about a nonprofit component of their business. I share it here because I love what they are doing, and because there are elements many small businesses could and should consider mirroring.

The program is called Cares4Kids. Any ConstantContact customer can nominate one children-focused not-for-profit organization to receive a free ConstantContact account. It's a simple, thoughtful, and powerful approach to community building and support.

Here's what I like about it. It helps organizations that need help. That alone is reason enough, but it also allows the customer to be the bearer of the gift. And, of course, the gift is the product. These three elements combine to make this a very powerful strategy.

Find ways to help your customers do good and spread the word about your product at the same time, and you've got a winner for all involved.

Word-of-mouth popcorn

When Andy Sernovitz sent me a review copy of his book, *Word of Mouth Marketing,* he shipped it in a very unique package. The book came in a small sample gift pack from the Dale and Thomas Popcorn company. The package contained a small bag of popcorn, a copy of the book, and, here's the kicker, a catalog of gift items from Dale and Thomas Popcorn. I'm guessing—I could be wrong, but it would still make sense—that Dale and Thomas paid the shipping for this mailing as a way to get in front of a targeted and chatty audience.

The referral partnership was a win for both parties, as it demonstrated a nice word-of-mouth tactic related to the book and got me to talk about the tactic both here and elsewhere.

The reverse-testimonial referral tactic

As we've covered in this book, acquiring testimonials from happy clients is a great way to get great content to sprinkle throughout your marketing materials. When prospects read credible comments from a satisfied customer, endorsing the promise of your marketing message, it has real impact.

I advocate asking every single client for a testimonial, whether you use them all or not, because I think it forces the client to consider the value you bring or, and this is equally important, it allows them to discuss why they don't feel comfortable providing you with a testimonial.

Pretty straightforward to this point, but now here's the reverse part.

When you receive a testimonial from a client, clip a very powerful sentence or paragraph and print a dozen postcards with your client's comment, a simple offer, and your contact information. Send this pack of cards to your client and ask them to jot a handwritten note on each one and send them along to folks they think would benefit from this offer. (Yes, put postage on the cards.)

The power of this little technique is that you have made yourself very easy to refer, you have personalized the referral, and you have created a marketing approach that may stir a little buzz from sender and receivers—all good things. Plus, any clients that send these out have just resold themselves on being a client.

Landing pages for referrals

Landing pages are pretty standard fare these days—you run an ad in a publication and drive people to a landing page specifically designed to generate one response only, whether that is to sign up for a newsletter, enroll in a teleseminar, or request a white paper.

What if you took this tool and designed a page on your Web site just for referrals? In other words, create a page that you would share with your clients and strategic partners that they could use as a tool to refer your business. Instead of telling a potential referral to check out your Web site, your referral sources would tell them to go to a specific page set up to personally greet them and acknowledge their status as someone who has been referred.

This simple personalization step allows you to speak directly to this special visitor, and even to go as far as give them a specific call to action. Knowing that your referral sources have this tool to use will also help make sure that the referrals you do receive are highly qualified.

You can take the idea to the next level. If you have strategic partners who routinely refer prospects, or ones who you would like to convince to routinely refer prospects, set up a page just for them. Feature their logo and a welcome message just for their referred visitors. Once you create the template for this type of page, there is no reason you can't create a dozen more to really add a professional touch to your referral process.

A passive referral system

This one comes from Scott Hensley of Affordable Concrete Cutting (www.affordableconcretecutting.com):

> I implemented what we call a passive referral plan, because I didn't really like to go out and ask for referrals, but I can say I get at least a hundred times the referrals now as I did before I had a referral plan. The power is in having a plan.
>
> I merged my referral plan into my marketing plan to some degree. I derive a lot of business from the yellow pages, and unfortunately, yellow pages people are loyal to the yellow pages, and the next time they need a concrete cutter they will return to the yellow pages and might wind up being serviced by my competition, or who I like to call the "uninsured toothless caveman."
>
> As a self-proclaimed marketing professional, I like to vision it as similar to the Old West; my competition and I are ranchers. These yellow page customers are wild cattle, and when they come up to one of my fences, I open the fence quickly and drag them in. I then take my branding iron and brand them. I send them to re-education training,

if you will. Everything that they see or hear in the next several days is "Affordable Concrete Cutting" and my logo, so I can gently hypnotize them into never even thinking of leaving my ranch, and when they call home or call their friends they tell everyone what a fantastic experience they have had here and how it would be great for their family, friends, and colleagues to join them.

On top of that, I keep my fences in tip-top shape by keeping in touch with my customers, by using USPS Direct Mail mailings every month or by sending them a decent gift for no reason other than to remind them of the great experience that they have had here.

My first contact with the customer is via a phone call inquiry. I mention my company name several times, and I make the customer feel great about using us. Next my guy goes to the site and performs the cutting. This is where the marketing and branding or rebranding begins. Once the job has been completed successfully, my men give the customer a paid invoice and ten or so business cards and . . . ask that they mention it to everyone.

We then send each customer a computer-generated paid invoice with an insurance certificate request form and a W-9. On the invoice I handwrite a thank-you, and I enclose several business cards and a Rolodex card.

In addition, I put a big sticker on the envelope that reads "Thank You! We appreciate your referrals." Then I prepare a thank-you card that basically says, if you were happy with our service then please tell everyone. I don't mail this until a day after I mail the invoice. Then I prepare a gift pack that contains a gift, a pocketknife with my logo on it, a mouse pad, [and] some pens or a couple of pads of paper.

Inside this mailing we enclose a bunch of business cards. Since I started using the stickers and the thank-you cards, as a system, my business has exploded and is increasing exponentially.

Create your own referral network

This idea comes from Walt Ford of ReferralNetworX (referralnetworx .com) in Pleasant Grove, Utah:

> About six months ago, along with my son, Alex, we decided to start our own referral group. I [had] been a member of several different groups previously but had some ideas of my own. We have successfully launched ReferralNetworX. We are more that just a lead-generation type of group. We are vested in the education of referral marketing.
>
> I am now running this endeavor alongside of my cleaning business. I have many great stories about how referrals have landed us huge accounts in the cleaning industry, but even more exciting are some of the stories that are beginning to emerge from our group!

Customers as mentors

This approach comes from Scott Valentine of Bisk Education Inc:

> Here is a referral project that should work for you: . . . [P]ut those that offer referrals on your payroll, by offering incentives and name recognition.
>
> The idea is to get your current customers to spread brand information through word-of-mouth marketing for free by offering mentoring opportunities. This strategy is probably most suited for products that are complicated, or require long-term use or reuse. Offering previous users an opportunity to mentor others helps shape the product experience while catering to the self-interest of the individual.
>
> It is really a win-win situation for both parties, and consumers feel they have more ownership of the product, since

they have a say in how it is perceived. This can, however, become a double-edged sword, and proper training and communication is required in order to ensure that consumers get the experience they desire.

It is not a challenge to get people [who] have a negative experience to communicate their displeasure, but it is a challenge to get those [who] have a positive message to communicate their experience to potential prospects; this is the vehicle that can deliver this experience.

Planned testimonial gathering for referrals

This tactic comes from Brent Sampson, CEO of Outskirts Press (www .outskirtspress.com):

> Word-of-mouth referrals and testimonial-generation programs have been one of the leading contributors to our company's rapid growth. We do a number of things, and, of course, it all depends upon giving our authors a positive experience so they *want* to recommend our services to others. That's very important. What good is having a referral program if customers don't want to refer you? So we invest a lot of resources into ensuring high customer satisfaction.
>
> Within one month of their publication date, we follow up with them with the specific goal of getting feedback from them. The first is a customer satisfaction survey, where we ask them about their experience and ask them to rank us in five categories. We also provide them a feedback form on this survey where they can include additional comments. A lot of our wonderful testimonials come from there, and we post many of our author testimonials throughout our Web site and on our marketing materials.
>
> A second correspondence after their book is published asks them specifically to provide a testimonial about their positive experience with Outskirts Press, and we point

toward the potential exposure their book could receive in exchange for taking the time to draft a comment. We've found it's beneficial to give them something to make up for the time investment they are making drafting a nice e-mail, but it doesn't always have to be in the form of money. But, money doesn't hurt either, so several months after their book is published, we notify them about our referral program and how they can earn a referral bonus (in the way of cash) for referring other authors to us.

We also have a customer loyalty program for our top-of-the-line publishing package, where they can receive a 10 percent discount if they return to publish with us again.

The results have been outstanding. We receive so many positive comments as a result of tactics number one and number two described above that we don't have the resources to include all the positive comments we receive on our Web site. And in terms of tactic number three, we find that many of our authors refer us to their associates and friends/family of their own accord, long before hearing about our referral program. And even after they hear about it, it doesn't change their motivation. When you make a customer happy, they discover that referring others is its own reward.

Provide extreme value

This series of steps come from Jamie Glass, President of Artful Thinkers, LLC (www.artfulthinkers.com):

As a small business owner, I found that my best clients come from existing clients or people [who] I have worked with at other companies. In three years, I have only taken one client [who] came from a Web site inquiry. I found people want to do business with someone [who] has integrity and they can trust. This is validated when you are referred by a former colleague or existing client. My tips are below.

In short, my best tips are: provide *extreme* value, join a group with someone you can tailgate, and provide pro bono work.

Here are my tips:

1. If you provide value to your clients, you don't have to ask for referrals—they come because they are proud of their association. I remind my clients of the value that they get when we work on projects, and always focus on ROI, to show them we are on the same team. This resonates and is often the message they repeat to the people they refer to me.

2. I join local business groups and associations so people see my name all the time *and* I will only join when I know someone else in the group [who] is a power networker and has great influence in the group, so they can make the right introductions. I call this tailgating. It shortcuts the get-to-know-you stages. I often get, "I know you . . . I know Artful Thinkers."

3. I provide pro bono work to groups that have a big circle of influence. I try to have three pro bono clients at one time. The volunteer aspects often lead to other business opportunities. I volunteered to do PR for an alumni club in Phoenix and got a paying client in twenty days [through] one of the club membership leaders.

4. My clients know me as a member of their team. I speak in "we" and "our," not "I" or "me."

5. I always offer strategic purpose to the tactical solutions. It helps people know that I understand their goals and what they want to achieve.

6. When I am referred, I follow-up immediately. I also respond back to the referring person with a thank-you and the next steps. They feel proud and involved in the handoff.

7. I offer a sixty-minute evaluation that is usually packed with tips and advice that reference the work I do with people they know. They are often hungry to join the club.

Making referrals a community event

This idea comes from Sara Fontanez of Fontanez Photography in Plano, Illinois, and it was submitted by her printer, Vistaprint (www .vistaprint.com):

> Like most small businesses, her marketing budget is tight and she can't spend advertising dollars like a large company. Because she photographs many different things, including people and their pets, she coordinated a pet photography day called "Pets & People—Paws for Pics" to raise her visibility and acquire new customers locally. A local groomer cosponsored the event with her and allowed Sara to use her facility. The two businesses promoted the event using postcards purchased for under fifty dollars.
>
> At the event, both businesses showcased their services and marketing materials, which enabled them to both meet and acquire new customers. Through this event, Sara was introduced to several other small businesses related to the pet industry, like vets, sitters/walkers, and homemade dog food vendors.
>
> Marketing materials, such as brochures and business cards, were collected ahead of the event from each of the participating vendors for a "doggy bag" for customers to take home with them.
>
> Because the doggy bag concept was such a success, Sara has taken it to a new level. Now all of the small businesses are coordinating efforts to produce four thousand of these bags to distribute to local homes. In the bag is a postcard or rack card from each company (none of which are direct competitors), a business card with each company's contact information, and a raffle ticket. Not only do customers now have their contact information, but they are encouraged to

call each company listed in the bag to see if they've won a prize. Everyone had agreed to donate five prizes.

And since many of the businesses involved already had postcards and printed marketing materials, the cost was minimal. With creative thinking, Sara has taken a simple campaign and evolved it into a true communitywide partnership that can benefit each business as well as many customers.

Systematic follow-up for referrals

This simple but powerful concept comes from Vince Golder, managing director of Goldnet Referral Marketing Ltd (http://www.goldnetrefer ralmarketing.co.uk/) from a question I posted on LinkedIn:

> My wife and I went out one day a few years ago to buy a new lawn mower and ended up buying her a new car!!! The salesman, by the name of Wayne, asked our permission to contact us by phone three times over a six-month period, and he broke this down to calling us within one week, four weeks and six months of the purchase.
>
> He stated quite clearly [that] the only reason for contact was to simply check if we are still happy with my wife's car, and if we had any problems he would get them sorted ASAP. I must admit I was very skeptical that Wayne would do this, but I kept an open mind. Guess what? Wayne did exactly as he said, and over this period we gave him eleven referrals, six of whom he made sales to, and we also got vouchers worth three hundred pounds [$499.23 in 2009 U.S. dollars] toward paying for car servicing and accessories.
>
> Wayne indirectly encouraged us to give him many referrals because he proved he sincerely cared about us through his customer communication program, and he got us to think more about him and the quality service he gave us,

plus we trusted he would give the same benefits and value to people we referred.

Those three calls the salesman made to us earned him and his company approximately £125,000 [$208,016.93 in 2009 U.S. dollars] of business for little cost and effort. If he had not called us, it is very unlikely we would have given him any referrals; this basic but powerful strategy of customer follow-up and care and communication can be easily applied by most businesses.

Most businesses miss out on huge business potential due to a lack of a simple follow-up strategy such as Wayne operated. They try and chase business from cold prospects with all the challenges that incurs, when all the business they can handle can be available via their customers, quickly, simply, and at very little cost.

CHAPTER 12

Snack-sized Suggestions

While I maintain that most referral strategies can be applied in some fashion to almost any type of business, there are some that are more suitable to certain kinds of businesses than others.

In this chapter I have taken a host of tactics and examples and aligned them with the appropriate retail, service, and professional services categories. Most of these "snack-sized" ideas are fairly generic in nature and simple to execute, but the intent of this chapter is to get you thinking about multiple ways to fill in some gaps you might have in your referral tactics, and to get your brain working on some creative approaches once you have your foundational systems in place.

All of the examples given here were taken from real-life businesses I have encountered through speaking to, reading about, and meeting with small-business owners from around the globe.

Retail

Gift store (Frequent Referral Club)—Set up a frequent referral club that rewarded customers for sending in referrals. Every time a customer made a purchase they were given a referral certificate good for twenty dollars off a one-hundred-dollar purchase. When that certificate came back in the store, the referral customer also earned points toward free items.

Computer store—Had an associate write some simple but useful software programs. The store then gave them away freely and asked customers and users to do the same. Each program required a simple registration to install, and each time someone used the program they were greeted with information on store specials. The store received thousands of subscribers and impressions as users passed the software around.

Clothing store—Partnered with surrounding, noncompeting stores to promote and refer each other. Each store created discount cards and displayed them in the store and inserted them into shopping bags. The stores also shared mailing lists and held "secret" afterhours specials, just for customers who referred business.

Hair salon—Routinely dropped of coded coupon and gift cards to area hotels. The staffs at hotels are constantly asked for advice on a nearby hair salons or other retail businesses. The hair salon even provided free services to hotel staff members that referred the most business.

Home décor store—This store compiled a list of the most popular items in the store, and when a customer purchased this item they received a gift card to give to a friend for another popular item.

Optical store—Offers new clients a 100 percent refund if they refer four new clients within one year. Obviously the math works out for them, but business skyrocketed when they made this offer. They give their customers referral cards, and each time one of the cards comes back, they send a refund check to their customer. When customers reach four new referred clients, they have received a 100 percent refund for their previous purchase. They find that their customers get pretty excited about the prospect of "winning the game" and are driven by this competition to refer new clients. Of course they have photos of the 100% Refund Club all over the office.

Independent bookstore—Teamed up with neighborhood schools to start a reading program. Students were encouraged to read a certain number of books that they checked out at the library. Each time the book was read the student received a punch on a reading card. After they filled up their card they received a free book from the bookstore. This promotion got the bookstore tons of publicity and exposure from the library and the school. Being smart marketers, they also were able to acquire the books they gave away from the remainders section offered by publishers. Typically this partnership arrangement allowed the bookstore to get the giveaway books, still high-quality, desirable books, for under one dollar.

Plumbing supplies store—Offered salespeople from plumbing and other construction-related firms finders' fees for giving his salesperson leads. A painting contractor would give him a heads-up when he was asked to bid a job, and then the plumbing supply contractor could reach out and make a special offer to the homeowner or contractor. If the lead turned into a job, he would send a check to the salesperson from the other company. Having all of these paid scouts out there really kept him in the know about who was doing what.

Shopping center—Created a discount card that offered discounts and specials for every store in the mall and contacted area sports teams, religious groups, and schools and allowed them to give the cards away to members. When a member came to the mall and used the card, the group received a certain percentage of the proceeds.

Golf driving range—When members signed up for a package that includes ten sessions, they got four "Free Range Time Coupons" to give out to others who they would like to bring to the club. They found that 35 percent of these free players returned and paid.

Home sales—Clients picked out a lot and the model of the home they were interested in building, but before they could write the check for the deposit, they had to provide five referrals. After they were sold, they literally wouldn't take their money unless they complied.

Service businesses

Electrical company—Each time a service technician made a call they gave the customer five five-dollar referral-bucks certificates. The certificates had the customer's name on them. Customers were encouraged to give them to friends, family members, and neighbors. Each time one of those five-dollars-off coupons was used, the customer who gave them away also got a five-dollars-off coupon sent to them to use on their next service.

Mortgage company—Set the table ahead of time by showing clients exactly how he was going to perform. He set the cost savings, interest savings, and time frame for the transaction, all ahead of time. Then he got the client to agree to give him five referrals on the spot if he performed as promised. It became a game, and the clients always loved it. Plus, it pushed him to perform and emphasized the value he provided.

Computer consultant—He provided a service that was hard to explain and was best done in conjunction with a hardware upgrade. He joined an industry association and marketed his service exclusively as an add-on to the hardware upgrades. He provided a very specialized service, and many of the members in the organization were happy to refer him so they didn't have to mess with the service. He spent all of his time marketing to this industry referral source and acting as an extension of their businesses rather than trying to find end users.

Massage therapist—Every time a new client signed up for their six-session package, they got three referral cards for a free massage. Clients gave the cards away to friends and family. If one of those free massage cards then turned into a six-session buyer, the original client got a free massage.

Computer repair—This company simply asked for referrals every time they marketed or communicated with their clients in any manner. They created a big rubber stamp that said "We crave referrals" and stamped that sentiment on every piece of mail that left the place. Invoices, marketing pieces, newsletters, training manuals, work orders . . . you name it. By putting that message in front of their prospects constantly, they began to receive referrals from many different places.

Heating and air conditioning contractor—During the sales process they used testimonial letters from satisfied clients and then asked the clients if they would be willing to provide a similar letter if everything worked out as promised. The customers and technician agreed on a quoted price, the technician completed the work, and then before collecting payment, offered an additional fifty-dollar referral fee if the clients wrote a letter on the spot. It worked every time.

Mortgage company—This company acquired rosters from area private schools and then solicited business using these rosters and offered to provide his services for free to any borrower who would send a mailing to the entire school's parents endorsing the company's services. The fee the company gave up was almost one thousand dollars, but in most cases the mortgage company immediately signed up as many as ten new clients, and the owner became known as the go-to person in these tight-knit communities. This works well with church groups, associations, and clubs as well.

Painting contractor—A great paint job takes more than luck. He worked very hard at generating referrals, and when someone would send him one he sent a handwritten thank-you note with a lottery ticket enclosed. He got a ton of mileage from the stunt, and it helped reinforce his core message.

Software training company—Partnered with complementary businesses to provide training classes. A local print shop received all kinds of very poorly designed business cards, brochures, letterhead, etc. It partnered with a computer training company to offer its customers graphic design classes. Eventually they expanded it to marketing, Web design, and specific software applications. The key is to look for businesses where you can offer a natural extension of their product or service.

Lawn service—Created a referral group of complementary services—tree service, plumber, heating and cooling, window cleaning, maid, driveway repair, handyman. Then each of the services marketed the entire group with dollar-off coupons whenever they did work or made a marketing call on a homeowner or business.

Remodeling contractor—After this upper-end remodeling contractor finished a project, he offered to throw an open house party for friends and neighbors. The homeowner invited everyone to "come see what all the fuss was about" and see the new home. The remodeling contractor made a very small presentation and then passed out cards. This worked particularly well when he added a cigar tasting, a wine tasting, and a golf demonstration to the event. Of course, he also took photos of the homeowners enjoying their new home addition and mailed it around the neighborhood.

Sales trainer—Offered an all-expenses-paid trip to Cancún for the person who referred the most clients in a year. Contests have been around forever because they work. They had many different levels of prizes, and even gave a little something whenever they received a refer-ral, even if the referral did not turn into a client.

Remodeling contractor—Sent a series of letters to houses surrounding a project. This way they let the neighbors know what was going on, gave them contact informa-tion, and promised to keep the job site as tidy as pos-sible. But the real thing they were doing was sending a powerful marketing message that said, "look how much we care about our customers." The final letter included a photo of the completed project and a quote from the happy homeowner.

Electrical contractor—Paid its salespeople twenty dollars for every referral they generated. They put door hangers on ten or so houses surrounding a job they were working on. When one of the coupons on the door hanger came in, that salesperson got twenty dollars. The key was that the door hanger had the address of their customer listed on it, saying something like "We were working at 1233 Mockingbird Lane today, and we thought you might like a twenty-dollars-off coupon for any electrical ser-vice you may need." This personalization is what makes this a referral-type strategy.

Maid service—Sent out fake one-hundred-dollar bills as a Valentine's Day gift to all of its clients and then allowed them to gift this one hundred dollars off their service to anyone they wanted. They acquired new clients, and their existing clients felt great about being able to give this valuable gift away.

Window-washing company—Most of their clients were so pleased with the way their clean windows looked, they actually felt compelled to tip the crew. Whenever that happened, the crew chief handed over three refer-ral postcards and asked the client to address them and place a note on them right on the spot. The crew chief then mailed the cards for the client. They got one in three of these back as a new client.

Seminar company—Let clients come back to a seminar for free if they brought one paying guest. They made money on products that they sold, and they felt that this offer actually helped sell people in the first place.

Auto dealer—A day or two after a client bought a new car, the auto dealer sent a very large (hard to miss) balloon bouquet to the client's office. He found that everybody in the office insisted on knowing who sent the balloons. He always gots calls on this one.

Wedding photographer—Offered couples a free portrait ($250) on their one-year anniversary if the couples would provide three referrals at the time of the wedding. Then they also asked the couple for the list of the entire wedding party and sent them thank-you notes for being so helpful with all of the arrangements, photos, etc. The photographers also offered a free family photo as a way of saying thanks. What they found was that people who were in wedding party soon married as well.

Independent professionals

Financial planner—Created his very own referral and lead network by sending a letter to ten other professionals whom he had worked with and felt comfortable referring business to. This letter informed them that he was creating a unique referral network of one hundred of the area's top professional services providers and was inviting them to become a member, but that he needed them to recommend ten others who should belong to this exclusive group. He then created a resource directory and Web site that featured all one hundred professionals. The entire group promoted the directory and Web site and referred business to each other. As a result, other professionals begged to be allowed into the group. The strategy was so powerful that many of network members did no other form of marketing.

Business consultant—Every time he acquired a new client he took his/her photo and made postcards for him/her to send to referrals. The photo made the card much more effective and generated much better referrals.

Attorney—Sponsored online teleseminars and invited well-known authors and speakers by allowing them to pitch their books or other products. Targeted clients lined up to hear the prominent speaker and provided their names and e-mail addresses to get on the free call. The teleseminars became so popular that the attorney recorded each call and created an entire library of products that he used for other marketing efforts. By sponsoring the well-known authors, the attorney created a very high-profile referral network.

Dentist—Created what he calls compliment cards: Every time a client gave a compliment, like "That didn't hurt at all" someone on his staff was ready with a referral card. The staff also emphasized that the only way they work is by referral.

Marketing consultant—Contacted a bank and an accounting firm that both had small-business clients and offered to put on a free marketing seminar for their clients. The bank and the accounting firm invited the guests and provided the space and refreshments. The marketing firm provided the seminar content. The bank and accounting firm liked the idea of doing something for their clients, but the twist that really made this work was that the bank and accounting firm saw it as an opportunity to meet each other's clients and perhaps get some good exposure to prospective clients.

Management consultant—This smart marketer made it a habit of acquiring testimonials from every single client he had ever worked with. In some cases he had testimonials from every single person that worked for a business he had consulted with. At some point, he had more than five hundred letters from thrilled clients. Then, when a prospective client would call and ask for information on his company or request a proposal for services, he would simply create a spiral-bound five-hundred-page book of testimonials with a snappy cover and send it over. The prospects were floored by so much proof.

Business coach—At networking events people would always ask how business was, and he would typically respond something like, "Just great." Now he simply says, "Business is very good, but I am always looking for more clients who need this . . ." Then he hands them a referral card that clearly states the types of issues, challenges, and frustrations that he helps people through. Just changing his response to this seemingly automatic question has changed the way he generates referrals.

Financial planner—Does fee-only work and states that part of the fee is that the client must provide five referrals. After working with a client for a few months he was able to learn a lot about what they do, what clubs they belong to, what religious organization, etc. He then created a customized list of prospects he knows he wants as clients who his new client may know. Then, instead of simply asking the client if he/she knew anyone else who needs planning services, the financial planner put a list of fifty or so highly targeted names in front of the client and got great referrals every single time.

Insurance broker—Once a month this broker invited his most important referral sources to lunch and had them picked up at their offices by a limo service. This little ploy made his referral sources feel special, but, perhaps more important, it forced them to explain to their associates why the limo was waiting for them. This word-of-mouth buzz sent a lot of other would-be referral generators his way.

Marketing consultant—He put on a free seminar and then offered another free seminar on an even hotter topic to everyone in the room who would come back in a week and bring two other business owners. He went from thirty participants to ninety with no additional marketing.

Insurance sales—This insurance agent turned his business-owner clients into stars. He interviewed some of his highest-profile clients on what it took to be successful in business. He recorded these interviews and eventually turned them into a very useful business-building library. Then he sought out potential interview guests to include in the series. These business owners didn't see him as an insurance salesperson; they saw him as a member of the media who had the ability to offer their business lots of free publicity. But, eventually, many of these featured businesses bought insurance from him and, in all cases, they promoted his business when they gave away or sold the library of interviews.

Construction consultant—Over the years this construction consultant had created about fifty construction-related publications and training guides. They had offered the books through direct sales on their Web site or at trade shows. Then they decided to launch an affiliate program that allowed every trade association and industry group to promote their products for a share of the revenue. The entire process was automated, using the Internet, and each of the participating affiliates had a unique URL that allowed it to promote the books. There are many companies selling product this way on the Internet, but this was still fairly unique in this industry, and the sales were astonishing. Any business can take advantage of this approach—no matter what you sell.

Financial planner—Created a marketing board of directors to review and suggest ways to better market his services. The group was wisely chosen, in some cases for their ability to refer target clients. After joining a formal board structure, they became very invested in the success of the business, and became very active referral sources. The format also allowed them to completely understand how to sell the business, so the leads they attracted were exactly the right kinds.

Accounting firm—In an effort to increase business with dental practices, this accounting firm approached a well-respected dentist and convinced him to let them take over certain aspects of his accounting at no charge. In exchange, the dentist would send a letter to the entire dental society in his town recommending the accounting firm's services. Of course it goes without saying that the accounting firm needed to perform as promised. The program was so successful that it eventually grew to add legal, financial, and marketing consultants and offered a half-day seminar sponsored by the initiator. This dentist gained tremendous exposure from the partnership.

Attorney—Held Friday help clinics on a range of nonlegal issues every Friday from 2:00 P.M. to 4:00 P.M. He would allow clients to call in and get free help related to the chosen topic of the week. Another professional expert provided the assistance. One week it might be tax issues from an accountant, the next it was environmental issues, then marketing, then HR. The idea here was that his clients saw it as a great way to get some very specific free help and the other professionals saw it as a great way to get in front of some prospects.

Marketing consultant—Partnered with a local business newspaper that agreed to sponsor his seminar. The seminar topic was very appealing, and the cost for the seminar was $149. The consultant gave 50 percent of the fees to the newspaper in return for an all-out promotional campaign in print. The newspaper covered all of the ad costs, the consultant filled up the seminar and made a good profit, but he really benefited from the credibility that the sponsorship generated.

Financial planner—Clients would come in for an annual review and he would surprise them with something very nice and very unexpected. While the client sat in the planner's office looking out the big picture window, a mobile automobile detail service would arrive and detail the client's car. Clients were so pleased, they talked about it for a week to everyone they met. He initiated this as a client service, but he found that he got so much word-of-mouth support from it that it turned into a referral system. Every year he tries to outdo the last, and his clients can't wait for their annual review meeting.

Public relations firm—The first meeting with a new client always involves a homemade cherry pie. The cherry pie fits with a theme of their marketing, but the effect is that it creates lots of good will and buzz. Food is a good referral tool.

Law firm—Contacted the board members of almost every local charity in their town and offered to host their board meetings at their offices. The law firm had a very nice conference room with plenty of media tools, and the firm offered drinks and copies as part of the deal. Several large organizations without good meeting spaces took it up on the offer. The members of the boards of those large organizations were exactly the business owners and leaders that the law firm wanted exposure to. This gave them a built-in marketing process after they were willing to make such a generous contribution to the charities.

Accounting firm—Produced several very easy-to-understand guides for certain types of tax situations people found themselves in, such as divorce, an IRS audit, college tuition, and starting a new business. They used these reports in their marketing efforts but also offered them free of charge to lawyers, financial planners, and other consultants who had clients that might appreciate and need this kind of information. In some cases they offered to cobrand the materials by putting the law firm name and logo on the covers of the booklets along with their own information. The law firm got additional marketing materials and the accounting firm got referrals.

Dentist—Installed an oven and small kitchen in his office and baked chocolate chip cookies every day. Every patient left with a little gift bag of cookies. A couple of things made this work so well. Instead of smelling like a dental office, the place smelled wonderful. The cookies were really good, so people appreciated getting them, and the practice was so unique that people naturally talked about it to friends and associates.

CHAPTER 13

Workshop

At the end of Chapters 5 through 10 I posed the following action ideas. I've grouped them here in the form of a workshop to make it easier for you to think holistically about building your entire plan.

While there are many foundational elements to consider, your planning process will eventually unfold in these six elements of your business, marketing, and referral system.

1. Your strategy action plan
2. Your content action plan
3. Your convergence action plan
4. Your direct customer network plan
5. Your indirect partner network plan
6. Your ready-to-receive action plan

By completing, or at least outlining, the various elements of these six core widely referred business elements you can begin to experience the systematic momentum that's necessary for long-term business growth.

Your strategy action plan

I know there was a lot in these chapters, so before we move on, let's recap and create a list of action steps for thinking about, planning, and creating your authentic strategy.

The higher purpose—Can you identify a sense of mission that ultimately drives why your organization does what it does? Not a mission statement—a purpose.

Nobody does that—What is the talkable innovation that you are going push out into the market as a clear demonstration of your unique way of doing business?

The core difference captured—What simple phrase, metaphor, or slogan can you create to simplify and quickly communicate what your core difference is?

Visualizing the ideal customers—Can you start to formulate precisely what an ideal customer or customer segment looks like?

The key story—What is the simple truth contained in your primary marketing story? Can you utilize this story to help illustrate what makes your organization unique?

Leader as storyteller—How can you teach and keep the story as an integral part of your organization's culture?

Referral brand elements—What imagery, identity elements, processes, and small flourishes will you use to further communicate the essential differentiation and core marketing message?

The secret sauce—What unique process of approach to doing business is going to act as the lever for delivery on your key point of differentiation?

The technology of delegation—What tools will you use to empower everyone in the organization to collaborate in the success of the customer experience?

Open book management—What set of numbers and key indicators do you need to teach and track in order to help everyone in the organization understand how the business grows?

Staff: blocking and tackling—What exercises, scorecards, and processes do you need to create and utilize to keep the elements of your authentic strategy top of mind and evolving with the entire staff?

Customer success quotient—Create the indicators and processes needed to capture the ultimate measure of marketing success—customer results.

Your content action plan

As we did in Chapter 5, now is a great time to pause and think through much of what we covered in this chapter.

Your killer "technology"—What is the secret sauce or way of doing business that you plan to use to drive your content strategy and key point of view for expanding your core difference?

Point-of-view white paper—What is the primary topic or outline for your point-of-view white paper?

Testimonial-gathering plan—How do you plan to gather testimonials from every happy customer?

What really triggers a referral—What customer phrases are important indicators of a need for what you offer?

Advertising for buzz—How can you utilize advertising to create awareness for your content?

PR for buzz—What is your plan for building relationships with key journalists to build awareness for your content?

Speaking for buzz—What topics, either trending or from your point-of-view white paper, would make great opportunities for you get in front of audiences?

Teaching business behavior—What behavior or practice would you like to teach your customers and prospect to better understand?

Blend and repurpose—How many different ways can you use and reuse the content you create?

Your convergence action plan

Wow, lots of information overload again. My hope is that while you've come to this point in our journey thinking big picture and strategically, you've also started to implement and act on some items you've discovered. But, once again, let's pause and scratch out an action plan for this important topic of convergence.

Hub and spoke, online and off-line—If your primary Web site is your content hub, where will you create spokes to your ideal clients?

The changing face of being found—What is your plan to optimize your content, including audio, video, and profiles?

Networking redefined—How will you merge the authentic aspects of traditional networking with the opportunities that exist in social networking?

Lead nurturing is personal—What technologies, campaigns, and personal touches can you bring to the process of moving a lead from know, like, and trust to try and buy?

Blog as convergence generator—What is your plan to create and optimize a blogging tool as your primary content and convergence generator?

Multiple blog authors—How and when can you get customers, partners, and staff also creating content on behalf of your convergence strategy?

Podcast and become a journalist—Who could you interview and record as a content and convergence tool?

Audio as a customer service tool—How can you employ technology to get your customers involved in creating content and providing customer service?

Make video an everyday marketing activity—How will you take advantage of the growing effectiveness and expectation of video content?

Solve problems publicly—How can you move customer service and sales questions out into the public view?

Listening in a digital age—What items belong on a dashboard that allows you to monitor all that is being said about your brand?

A social media system example—What social media activities could you create routines around?

Your customer network action plan

What's your referral number?—How will you gauge the level of referral participation present in your customer base?

Lead conversion for referrals—What process will you use to introduce referrals as a condition of doing business with your organization?

Customer bill of rights—How will you communicate what rights and expectation your customer should have as part of a relationship with your firm?

Exceed expectations—What flourishes or surprises can you build systematically into your customer fulfillment processes?

The ultimate measure of marketing success—How will you measure, quantify, and communicate the success or results your customers obtain through your products and services?

Status updates—What mechanisms will you employ to communicate frequent and consistent status updates with your customers?

Reward champions—How will you acknowledge and reward your customer referral champions?

Equipping the team—What tools and processes will you need to build and employ to make it easier for your champions to refer business to your organization?

The highly engaged referral—How can you engage your customers to participate in the referral process at the most personal level?

Everyone's in customer service—What mechanisms, training, and mind-set are necessary to ensure that everyone in the organization is delivering customer service in line with the overall brand strategy?

Your strategic network action plan

Identifying your indirect team—Who belongs on your strategic partner team and how will you identify more?

Invitation to join—What process will you employ to help strategic partners view working with you as a direct benefit to them?

How to activate your network—What content cobranding, workshop, joint marketing, or creative partnership ideas will you employ to get your network active?

The fully engaged network—How will you structure and fully promote a more formal group of partners?

Teach your network well—What tools and tactics will you create and employ to teach your network partners how to be better referral generators, and to generate more referrals for themselves?

Make-a-Referral Monday—What tactics can you devise to keep the focus on giving referrals for all in your indirect network?

Your ready-to-receive action plan

How to frame a referral request—How will you position your requests for referrals in a manner that offers your referral source the benefit of doing so?

What a referral can tell you—What process will you create to ensure that you understand why every referral source recommends your organization?

How to give a referral—What process will you create to ensure that you are making referrals as effectively as receiving them?

Involve your employees in the referral engine—How can you get every employee involved in the acquisition of referrals?

Fix the follow-up—What processes will you need to create to properly and effectively follow up with your referred leads and your referral sources?

Communicate the progress—How will you track, capture, and communicate the progress and results you achieve on behalf of your referred leads?

Thank publicly—What tools and processes will you utilize to acknowledge and appreciate your referral sources?

Index

Creating Customer Evangelists
(McConnell and Huba), 152
customer(s):
accountability of, 162
asking what they value about your
company, 72, 100
average dollar transaction per, 88–89
becoming total resource for,
156–57, 159–60, 175
bill of rights for, 153–54
champion, 165–66
collaboration with, 50–51
communicating with, 162–65
cost of acquiring, 88, 89
employees as, 15–20, 87
expectations of, 47, 149, 157–58
feedback from, 112
ideal, 44, 55–56, 60–61, 72, 174
ideal, visualizing, 73–76
life cycle of, 44–48, 148
lifetime value of, 150–52
memberships for, 158–59
as mentors, 206–7
monthly introduction process for,
155–56
new customer kits for, 153–54, 155
owners as, 58–59
owner's manuals for, 154–55
prospective, 44, 50
referral toolbox for, 166–67
reviews by, 164
starter kits for, 155
staying connected with, 165
testimonials of, 98–99, 191, 202–3,
207–8
touch point map for, 48–49
customer network, 62, 148–73
action plan for, 172–73, 231–32
building communities, 170–71
champions in, 165–66
community space and, 171–72
friction and, 152–53
lead conversion and, 150
lifetime value and, 150–52
memberships in, 158–59

customer service, 172
customer success quotient (CSQ),
160–61

Dale and Thomas Popcorn, 202
dashboard, 20–21
delegation, 85–86
Delicious, 112, 122
Dell Computer, 133
dentists, 221, 226
differentiators, 55–60, 70–72, 94, 156
capturing, 73
Digg, 122
Digital Nomads, 133
Dimdim, 140
Dip, The (Godin), 7
DIY Marketers, 9–10
Duct Tape Marketing, 7, 95, 136

educational talks and workshops,
106–10
education-based marketing, 61, 92–94
see also content
electrical company, 216
electrical contractor, 219
eLunches, 139–40
e-mail, 52–53, 86, 117
E-mail Center Pro, 52–53, 86
emotion, 5–6, 32, 77–78
employees:
as brand element, 81
collaboration with, 52–53
as customers, 15–20, 87
empowerment of, 19–20, 30
hiring, 16, 17–18
open book management and,
20–21, 86–89
as owners, 22–23
in referral process, 190–91
training, 18–19, 89
*E-myth, The: Why Most Small
Businesses Don't Work and What
to Do About It* (Gerber), 97
E-Myth Worldwide, 97
Endline, Sarah, 18–19, 69, 80–81